PRECIOUS METAL

INVESTING AND COLLECTING IN TODAY'S
SILVER, GOLD, AND PLATINUM MARKETS

www.whitman**books**.com

PRECIOUS METAL

Investing and Collecting in Today's Silver, Gold, and Platinum Markets

ISBN 0794833993

Authored in the United States of America

Printed in the United States of America

Whitman Publishing is a leader in the antiques and collectibles field. For a catalog of related books, supplies, and storage products, visit Whitman Publishing online at www.whitmanbooks.com.

CONTENTS

FOREWORD

A Commentary on Precious Metal

Gold! Silver! The elusive precious substances have fired the imagination of mankind for centuries. To these have been added, in more recent times, platinum, palladium, and other noble metals.

Jason and his Argonauts sailed in quest of the Golden Fleece. "And with the ever-circling years comes 'round the age of gold," the carol goes. Indeed, the highpoint in any environment, discipline, or culture is usually characterized as its *golden age*. And, no better code of personal conduct has been devised than the Golden Rule.

"Every cloud has a silver lining," goes the old saying, meant to cheer us up in troubled times. (Or, as P.T. Barnum put it as he separated fools from their money, "Every *crowd* has a silver lining.") A *silver bullet* is a quick cure to a vexing problem. Children lucky enough to hail from wealthy families are said to be born with *silver spoons* in their mouths. And any family's really *good* tableware—the kind put out when important guests are dining—is its *silver*.

In Herman Melville's novel *Moby Dick*, Captain Ahab mobilizes his crew to intense action by posting as a reward for the capture of the white whale a golden doubloon nailed to the ship's mast. Visions of El Dorado, a golden man in a golden lake, lured Spanish conquistadors to South America centuries ago. The golden fortunes of Croesus, Midas, and Montezuma are part of lore and legend. In the 19th century, when the admonition "Go West, young man!" was given, the object of the westward journey was gold.

A gifted speaker is said to have a *silver tongue*. He might also have a *sterling* reputation; and on a *silver anniversary* he celebrates 25 years of marriage, employment, or another important undertaking.

Gold and silver have formed the subjects for countless volumes and narratives

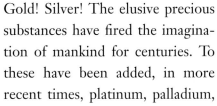

This hoard of electrum (silver/gold alloy) coins comes from ancient Ionia, in what is now Turkey. They are among the very first coins ever struck. (From *Milestone Coins: A Pageant of the World's Most Significant and Popular Money,* by Kenneth Bressett.)

ranging from journals of world discovery to exhortations to amass as much precious metal as possible in anticipation of doomsday.

As a glance at *Bartlett's Familiar Quotations* will easily verify, literature from the Bible down to the present day is strewn with innumerable references to gold. An interesting volume, *Gold the Real Ruler of the World*, by Franklyn Hobbs, published in 1941, gathered together many quotations, especially those with emphasis on the metal's monetary and financial value. Samples:

> "Gold is the cornerstone of the whole business and financial structure."
> "Gold is the key to the destiny of nations."
> "Gold is to commerce what the blood is to the body."
> "Gold is wealth, and the whole of wealth."
> "Gold is one of the greatest world forces that could be imagined."
> "No edict and no legislation can take the value out of gold."
> "The power of the Roman Empire waned as she lost her gold."

And the poignant "Gold is responsible for disagreement between men and wars between nations," as well as the philosophical "Gold is where you find it, but some of us never find it."

Shakespeare referred to gold many times, noting, for example that "The meat which made Caesar great was gold," and "Gold is the strength, the sinews of the world."

Sometimes golden dreams were tarnished, as the poet Robert Service related in a tale of the Klondike:

> I wanted the gold and I got it
> Came out with fortune last fall.
> Yet somehow life's not what I thought it,
> And somehow the gold isn't all.

Precious metals: they have fascinated us for millennia. They will continue to do so as long as we value rarity and beauty. With this book, you will learn how to profit in many ways from silver, gold, and other rare and precious elements.

Q. David Bowers
Wolfeboro, New Hampshire

Of all the world's treasures, gold is among the most prized.

1

WHAT IS GOLD, AND WHY IS IT VALUABLE?

For countless generations, gold has fascinated humankind and stoked our desire. For nearly 3,000 years we have prized it as a store of value and a means of monetary exchange.

In ancient Greece and Rome, gold coins were very important in commerce and trade as well as a way to accumulate wealth. In the years, decades, and centuries since then, gold has lost none of its appeal. Every civilized nation has recognized it as *the* standard of worth—easily traded between different countries, and, when properly assayed and evaluated, of standard international value.

Recently, gold has been very much in the spotlight around the world. In

Wealthy King Croesus of Lydia (c. 561–546 BC) introduced a type of gold coin called a *stater*. According to legend, Croesus's wealth came from gold found in the River Pactolus, where the mythical King Midas had washed away his golden touch.

This stater is shown enlarged. It is actually quite small, measuring only about 18 mm long (less than the width of a U.S. cent).

times of national economic uncertainty, international conflicts, and changing monetary values, gold gives us comfort. Sophisticated investors and financiers often consider it desirable to have a percentage of their assets in gold—a mental "break glass in case of emergency!" assurance.

In its most familiar form, gold is available in coins dating from ancient times down to the modern era. Coins of ancient Rome and Greece are necessarily rare and valuable. Later coins, too, from the Byzantine era,

Ancient Greek coins are rich in symbolism and history. This gold stater was issued in the name of Philip II of Macedon (the father of Alexander the Great). It might have been made to celebrate a chariot race that the king personally won in the Olympic Games. (shown 3x actual size)

On this gold distater struck in the name of Alexander the Great, the goddess Athena wears a triple-crested helmet in the Corinthian style. On the reverse, Nike holds a wreath of victory. (shown 3x actual size)

This gold aureus of Emperor Severus Alexander shows the most famous building of ancient Rome: the Colosseum. (shown 3x actual size)

The emperor Justinian II used a portrait bust of Christ on this gold solidus of the Constantinople Mint. Robert Wilson Hoge, in *Money of the World: Coins That Made History*, notes that "Jesus, who was raised in the household of a carpenter, appears as elegantly manicured and coiffed as any fashionable Byzantine courtier." (shown 3x actual size)

medieval times, and more recent centuries, are very highly desired by collectors. Specialists who seek these are known as *numismatists*. As with any aspect of art, antiques, or historical items, expertise is needed to answer two questions: "Is it authentic?" and "Is it valuable?" Fortunately, many resources exist to help you. You'll begin to learn about them in this book.

Among the most romantic gold coins, from pirate and treasure lore, are Spanish doubloons or eight-escudo coins, with an original face value of about $16 in terms of American dollars. These are very popular with collectors today. They were struck in different mints in the 1700s and 1800s, and many are still available, particularly from Mexico, Central America, and South America.

The United States struck gold coins for circulation for nearly 150 years. The first were minted in 1795, and the last in 1933. These coins, like Spain's doubloons, are desired by many collectors worldwide. Those made in the early years, through early 1834, are notably rare and valuable. Those minted

Legend has it that King Charles III of Spain secretly ordered the murder of the man who engraved the "rat-nose" portrait on this gold doubloon, or eight-escudos coin. (shown 2x actual size)

"Forty-Niners" flooded into California after gold was discovered there in 1848 and news spread about the region's rich metal deposits. The pioneers soon needed a way to convert their raw gold—pinches of dust, small nuggets, and flakes—into something easier to carry and spend. Privately struck gold coins were the answer.

since 1834 are more readily available, as a class, though with some rarities in addition to many common dates. Double eagles ($20 gold pieces), the largest regular denomination of U.S. coins, contain nearly a full ounce of gold; those of the mid- to late 1800s and early 1900s can be bought at a modest premium over their bullion value. They are very popular and in constant demand. Dozens of different dates can be collected for just a small increase over the value of the gold they contain.

In the early 1850s, in Gold Rush–era California, San Francisco jewelers George Baldwin and Thomas Holman were among the private individuals who saw the public's need for gold coins. Coins were easier to transport and to spend than gold dust, flakes, or nuggets. Their firm of Baldwin & Co. struck several kinds of gold coins, including the Horseman type seen here. If you own a nice specimen, don't sell it for its gold value alone (about $650 when gold is at $1,400/ounce). It can be worth $35,000 to $200,000 or more, depending on its condition. Beware, though, that counterfeits exist. (Actual size 27 mm)

Since 1986 the U.S. Mint has issued bullion-type gold coins as part of its American Eagle program and other bullion programs. These are available each year, in several designs, and have marked denominations of $5, $10, $25, and $50. The coins have 1/10th, 1/4th, 1/2, and 1 ounce of gold respectively, and are issued by the Mint at a price based on current bullion value plus a premium. (If gold is selling at $1,500 an ounce, obviously the one-ounce gold American Eagle is worth much more than its face value of $50!)

Many other countries issue gold bullion coins. Canada's Maple Leaf coins, Austria's gold pieces with musical motifs, Great Britain's sovereigns, China's coins with panda bears, Australia's koalas and kangaroos, and South Africa's krugerrands are among the most popular worldwide.

In 2009 the U.S. Mint struck a modern version of the famous 1907 Ultra High Relief $20 gold coin. The coin is shown here at an angle to illustrate its 4 mm thickness, the lettered edge, and the depth of its relief. A much lower relief was used for the $20 gold coins minted from 1907 to 1933.

This coin was struck at the West Point Mint. People bought it both as a collectible, and as a bullion coin—that is, for its 24-karat gold content. (actual diameter 27 mm)

GOLD FACTS

Gold is an element, No. 79 in the periodic table. Its symbol is Au, from *aureus*, the name of an ancient gold coin. Gold is classified as a metal and is also known as a coinage metal. It remains solid at temperatures up to 1,948 degrees Fahrenheit.

Its color is . . . well, *gold*, itself an adjective. Yellow with a hint of red, or light yellow-orange, is a good description.

The atomic weight of gold is 196.966569, making it one of the heaviest of metals. It's difficult to create a fake gold bar out of, for example, common low-value lead—because lead is lighter, and a gold-plated lead bar can be detected by its specific gravity.

Gold is the most malleable and ductile of all metals. A single ounce of gold can be flattened out to create 300 square feet of gold foil. It is the most impervious of the coinage metals, and thus a thin sheet of gold foil can protect the dome of Georgia's state capitol building in Atlanta against the elements of weather and pollution.

Georgia's "Gold Dome" is protected by a very thin but protective layer of the precious metal. Eight other state capitol domes (those of Colorado, Connecticut, Iowa, Massachusetts, Nebraska, New Hampshire, New Jersey, and Wyoming) are gold-plated.

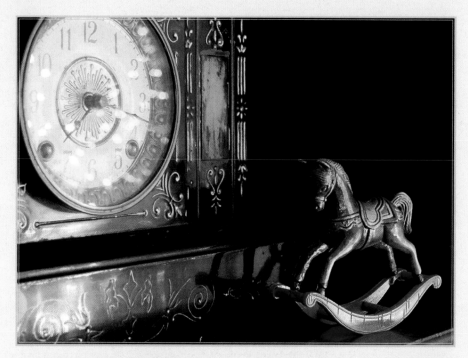

Gold leaf is used to decorate works of art.

For centuries gold has been used to create works of art and jewelry.

This ounce of gold is shown at actual size. If hammered into a thin foil, it could carpet a 15 x 20–foot room.

What Makes Gold Valuable?

Gold is a *precious metal*. The world's available supply is very small in relation to the demand for it.

Gold is used in coinage and ingots as a store of value, in jewelry (where it is the most prized and desired of all metals), and in commerce. Gold and gold foil are used in art and architecture, in electrical components and wiring, and, curiously enough, even in expensive foods and liquors.

Gold is valued on a per-ounce basis for the pure element. At regular intervals in London each trading day, the "spot" price is calculated. This number, a benchmark for trading, continually fluctuates. Sometimes the trend is downward, other times upward, and other times fairly flat. However, in the long term the value of gold has risen.

The world's largest gold bar, weighing 250 kilograms, in the Toi gold-mining museum in Japan.

Workers at the U.S. Mint, examining $100,000 face value of newly minted $20 gold coins (in the coiner's counting room of the Philadelphia Mint, January 1894).

In the United States, the Treasury Department officially valued gold at $20.67 per ounce from the early 1800s until January 30, 1934. After that it was pegged at $35. In the early 1970s the price was allowed to float freely and was no longer regulated. Since then, the trend has been upward. In 2009, for the first time ever gold crossed the $1,000 mark—and in 2010, it exceeded $1,400.

In commerce, dealers, brokers, and others charge a premium over the spot price when selling gold, and pay a discount under spot price when buying it. For ingots and newly issued bullion-type coins the margins are very narrow.

Gold is evaluated in terms of fineness. Pure gold is described as 1.000 fine, or, with the decimal omitted, as it often is, 1000 fine. Gold that is 90% pure is called 900 fine, and so on. The coinage for 19th and early 20th century American gold coins was 900 fine, with 10% copper and trace metals added to give the metal strength.

The value of gold depends on the demand for it.

In times of economic uncertainty, within a given nation the citizens will often prefer to hold gold instead of paper money. In the United States, paper money has no real monetary backing. It is offered on the "good faith and credit" of the government. A $100 bill cannot be exchanged at par for gold coins or those of any other precious metal. Instead, it can only be exchanged for, say, two $50 bills, or used to buy goods or services. When the stability of the American dollar is in doubt, demand for gold in the United States increases.

Gold as an investment medium has also fueled demand, this apart from its relation to paper money. Most countries, including the United States, have a reserve of gold bullion. Most of America's gold is stored in Fort Knox, Kentucky. When national gold reserves go down or are depleted, demand will increase worldwide.

This Series of 1882 $500 Gold Certificate (shown 63% of actual size) could be turned in to the U.S. Treasury in exchange for $500 face value in gold coins. Today's Federal Reserve Notes are not backed by gold.

Gold bricks stored at the United States Bullion Depository, Fort Knox, Kentucky. The fort is the world's single largest storehouse of gold, protecting nearly 150 million troy ounces of the precious metal.

The minting of gold commemoratives and bullion coins, and the fabrication of ingots, is an important industry and has contributed to international demand.

When demand decreases, such as when citizens of a country believe that their paper money has a more solid value, there will be less interest in buying gold. In times when money is scarce, such as during a recession or depression, fewer people will be able to buy gold.

Psychological factors also have an influence. Extensive advertising and publicity influence people to "like" gold. Holding gold offers a comfort level, a feeling of security. There is great satisfaction in viewing a collection of gold coins, or a stack of gold bullion coins, or a group of ingots.

The U.S. Mint made its first commemorative gold coins in 1903. Since then it has created hundreds of different kinds of gold coins and medals. (octagonal $50 coin shown actual size; all others enlarged 2x)

Gold is mentioned many times in fact and fiction, poetry, and elsewhere, and depicted in art. This adds to its allure, giving it a quintessential aspect that no other metal possesses.

International exchange rates also affect the price of gold, something that is rarely mentioned in discussions of the metal. If the value of the U.S. paper dollar drops 10% in relation to, say, the euro, gold will become more expensive for American citizens to buy, and the price in the United States will increase. At the same time, the price may remain stable or with little change in most European countries. If the dollar strengthens and rises 10% against the euro, the price per ounce of gold will decrease for American buyers.

Gold can be hidden away, to be brought out in hard times.

All that Glitters Is Not Gold!

"All that glitters is not gold." An interesting example of this is furnished by the "gold medals" awarded to exhibitors at the Louisiana Purchase Exhibition in 1904. This was to be the latest and greatest of the international fairs and important exhibitions held in America. The first American exposition of note was the Crystal Palace Exhibition of All Nations held in New York City in 1853. This was a privately financed venture housed in a huge glass-and-steel building near where the New York Public Library is today. Manufacturers, artisans, merchants, and others were invited to exhibit historical as well as contemporary items. Displays were judged, and prizes were awarded.

A beautiful medal—but is it solid gold? The savvy collector will do some research before making any precious-metal purchase. An example of this "gold medal" sold at auction in September 2009 for $805. If it had been solid gold, with its weight of three and a half ounces, it would have been worth more than $3,500.

In 1876 in Philadelphia the Centennial Exhibition was conducted in the vast expanse of Fairmount Park. Financed by the U.S. government and others, it consisted of many buildings, including those erected for states and foreign governments. Displays were judged, and honors bestowed, the highest being silver and gold medals. In the meantime the American Institute, based in New York City, had trade displays each year and awarded similar medals—but with the provision that once an item or product received a gold medal, if at a subsequent event it earned a similar award, only a paper "gold medal award" document would be issued, in order to keep the costs down.

The World's Columbian Exposition, planned to honor the 400th anniversary of Christopher Columbus's "discovery" of America, was to open in 1892, but delays took place and it was not until 1893 that the gates were thrown open. Again, there were awards galore, including gold and silver medals. The Trans-Mississippi Exposition in Omaha in 1898 and the Pan-American Exposition in Buffalo in 1901 were among the other events of this nature. Each featured large displays by merchants and manufacturers, and, again, silver and gold medals were awarded.

The main use of these honors was in advertising. Bottles of whisky, the fallboards on grand pianos, cases for jewelry, bottles of pepper sauce, and other products and packaging bore small images of the medals awarded, implying outstanding quality. In reality, many medals were awarded simply for showing up, so to speak—as an incentive for buying an expensive exhibit space. Without this attraction, many businesses would not have signed up.

Then came the Louisiana Purchase Exposition, popularly known as the St. Louis World's Fair. It was intended to open in 1903, but delays postponed the event until April 30, 1904. The fair continued until closing day on December 1, by which time about 20 million visitors had been counted. It was situated on a 1,272-acre tract in Forest Park in St. Louis. Fifteen major buildings, including four art palaces (one of which still exists today), formed the focus of the fairgrounds, with numerous smaller buildings, exhibit areas, fountains, gardens, and other attractions providing interest. Among the exhibits were many automobiles and other vehicles, demonstrations of wireless telegraphy, displays of the uses of electricity, and dirigibles. Works of hundreds of different artists, mainly painters, were on display.

Among the sculptors represented at the exposition were John Flanagan, Adolph A. Weinman, Evelyn Beatrice Longman, James Earle Fraser, Hermon A. MacNeil, and Daniel Chester French, all of whom would subsequently have connections with coin designs, commemorative or otherwise. One of them, Weinman, was commissioned to create award medals. Noted sculptors J.Q.A. Ward, Chester French, and the particularly famous Augustus Saint-Gaudens constituted the committee to work with Weinman.

The result was one of the finest medals ever created for an exposition. There was a little problem: the exposition desired to award a lot of gold medals—to the delight of exhibitors—but the medal was large and gold was expensive. The solution was simple and economically sound: prominently display the words GOLD MEDAL as part of the design, but strike the medals in copper alloy, and then gold plate them!

These beautiful "gold medals" may glitter, but they are not gold. All that glitters was not silver, either. The Louisiana Purchase Exposition's SILVER MEDALs were also only plated.

Collectors love them anyway, for they are truly magnificent works of medallic art.

In the composition of the obverse of the medal are shown two figures, one of which, Columbia, tall and stately, is about to envelop the youthful maiden by her side, typifying the Louisiana Territory, in the flag of the stars and stripes, thus receiving her into the sisterhood of states. The other figure is depicted in the act of divesting herself of the cloak of France, symbolized in the emblem of Napoleon, the busy bee, embroidered thereon. In the background is shown the rising sun, the dawn of a new era of progress to the nation.

The reverse of the medal shows an architectural tablet bearing an inscription giving the grade of the medal. Below the tablet are two dolphins symbolizing our eastern and western boundaries, the whole surmounted by an American Eagle, spreading his wings from Ocean to Ocean.

On the Gold Medal there are three distinct corners, each containing a wreath encircling a monogram or emblem, and each of these wreaths is surrounded by fourteen stars, representing the Louisiana Purchase States and Territories. On the Grand Prize design there is the same number of stars in the upper field of the shield, and there are thirteen bars in the lower field, representing the original States. On the design of the Silver Medal the artist has used the cross of the Order of Saint Louis.

The Medal was designed by Adolph A. Weinman. The design was approved by a committee composed of J. Q. A. Ward, Daniel C. French and Augustus St. Gaudens.

The dies were engraved and the medals struck by the United States Government Mint at Philadelphia. The alloy for the medals was made especially for the Exposition after samples were submitted and passed upon by expert medalists.

Since time immemorial, silver has been one of man's most treasured elements.

SILVER: GOLD'S LITTLE SISTER, VALUABLE IN ITS OWN RIGHT

S ilver is a basic element, with the chemical symbol Ag, derived from the Latin argentum, from the Indo-European root word *arg-* (for "grey" or "shining").

Silver has had many uses over the years, including in coinage, jewelry, and ornamentation such as tableware, vases, and works of art. In the 19th and 20th centuries silver was used in certain electrical wiring and contacts, in film and processing, and in medical and other applications.

This Cessna 210 was rebuilt for cloud seeding with a silver iodide generator. The inorganic compound is used to alter the composition of clouds to encourage rain.

A treasure hoard of beautifully crafted ancient silver tableware (dating to the first century AD) was discovered by Prussian soldiers in 1868. Pictured is the famous two-handled "Minerva bowl" from the Hildesheim hoard, now residing in the Altes Museum in Berlin.

The electrical conductivity of silver is higher than that of any other metal—even copper. (Silver's cost has prevented even wider employment in this regard, and copper became the metal of choice for most household and industrial wiring.) The melting point of silver is 961.78 degrees Centigrade, equivalent to 1,763.2 degrees Fahrenheit. Its density in solid form is 10.49. Silver is malleable, making it easy to convert into various forms and to stamp for coins and medals.

Silver is chemically active and will form compounds naturally. Coins, medals, silverware, and other struck, cast, and wrought silver objects will acquire tarnish or toning (sometimes attractive, sometimes not) over a period of time if subjected to the atmosphere.

Silver has often been compared to gold, and the prices of the two metals have often tracked each other, not in complete harmony, but relatively. In the 1700s and 1800s, various countries typically valued silver in a ratio to gold; for example, 15-1/2 or 16 ounces of silver would be worth one ounce of gold. Even a slight variation in the ratio caused problems from time to time; if silver became devalued, people would hoard gold, and vice versa.

Silver is found sometimes in native form (that is, in metallic form), but most often in combination with ores containing arsenic, sulfur, antimony, or chlorine. Silver is also a byproduct of the refining of ores of copper, lead, zinc, and nickel from certain localities, with Peru, Mexico, China, Australia, Poland, Chile, and Serbia being prominent.

In the United States, silver mining was a main commercial activity of the Western areas, particularly in Nevada (with its Comstock Lode), but also Utah, Colorado, and elsewhere. Nevada calls itself the Silver State. The industry was dynamic in the American West in the 1860s, resulting in great prosperity. In 1870 and continuing afterward, certain European countries and federations (the German Empire prominent among them) went off the silver standard for minting coins, and international demand dropped, as did the price. By the mid-1870s the silver-mining industry was

Silver-mining teams make their rounds in the boom town of Idaho Springs, Colorado.

European nations dump their "depreciated old silver" into the marketplace—"Uncle Sam's junk shop." (*Frank Leslie's Illustrated Newspaper,* June 7, 1879)

in deep trouble in the United States. The government tried to help, with the Coinage Act of 1873 providing for a new denomination, the trade dollar, intended for use in the Orient. At 420 grains of silver, the trade dollar was slightly heavier than the standard silver dollar at 412.5 grains. At

Production of the trade dollar propped up America's silver industry in the 1870s. The coin proved a commercial success in the Orient—especially in China, where merchants preferred silver to gold and refused paper money of any kind. (shown 1.5x actual size)

the time, China and India represented the two foreign countries in which there was a particularly great interest in silver. Production of the new coin helped American mining interests, but just to a small extent; the price continued to decline.

Finally, on February 28, 1878, Congress passed the Bland-Allison Act, mandating Uncle Sam to purchase millions of dollars' worth of silver bullion at market value each month, and to coin it into dollars. The problem

The Morgan dollar, named for designer George T. Morgan, was another boon to the nation's Western silver interests. "The coin's production [created] an artificial demand for the metal, whose market value had dropped sharply by 1878," notes the *Guide Book of United States Coins, Professional Edition*. "Today they are the most widely collected of all coins of their era." (shown 1.5x actual size)

was that silver dollars were not in wide use except in certain Western areas, and the quantities produced were far greater than needed by commerce. Hundreds of millions of new silver dollars piled up in Treasury vaults, banks, and other storage areas.

In the meantime, political interests arose, including the Greenback Party and the Free Silver movement. Activists thought that if the government would buy silver in absolutely unlimited quantities and turn it into coins, the Western economy would revive. This became the great political force of the late 1870s and 1880s, continuing into the 1890s, when it was the focal point of the presidential contest. William Jennings Bryan, the "Silver-Tongued Orator of the Platte," advocated government support of silver metal and was backed by many politicians and voters, particularly in the Midwest and West. They thought that money would become more readily available, and that cheaper dollars could be used to pay off mortgages and other debts. At the time the country was suffering from the Panic of 1893, which resulted in the closing of many businesses. Bryan's opponent, William McKinley, advocated gold as the monetary standard, as indeed it had been *de facto* (officially, the United States did not go on the gold standard until 1900, but that metal had been the foundation of

American coinage). Great debates ensued, and ultimately Bryan lost. The Free Silver movement and its adherents, called Silverites, faded, but not completely—in 1900 Bryan was back with the same campaign, but without as much interest. McKinley won again. Bryan threw his hat in the ring one more time, in the election in 1908, when he faced Republican contender William Howard Taft. However, silver was but a footnote in American politics by that time.

Choose Your Wage Standard.

WAGES ON THE GOLD STANDARD.

WAGES ON THE SILVER STANDARD.

As for example in U. S. and England, where necessities and even luxuries are within easy reach.

As for example in Mexico and India, where the workmen must go without the necessities of life.

William Jennings Bryan (seen here campaigning for the presidency in 1896) was strongly pro-silver. His opponents were convinced *gold* was the best standard for American coinage (as illustrated in the cartoon). "Disagreement over the monetary standard," writes Richard Doty in *America's Money, America's Story*, "gave late-1800s politicians much to argue about."

SILVER AS MONEY

Silver, more than gold, was the basis for American monetary transactions beginning in early colonial days. Indeed, the first coins minted within what is now the United States were the 1652-dated Massachusetts coins, from threepence to twelve pence, including the famous Pine Tree shilling of legend and lore. At that time, and continuing into the 19th century, a large amount of American commerce was done with Spanish silver eight-reales coins, or *pieces of eight*, that traded at the value of a dollar. When the Continental Congress first issued paper money in 1775, they were denominated in Spanish milled dollars. In addition, French, British, Dutch, German, and other silver coins were common in circulation and were legal tender for trade.

Massachusetts struck silver coins of various designs from the early 1650s into the early 1680s. Here are two types of "Pine Tree" shillings, dated 1652 but actually made years later. (shown 1.5x actual size)

Various foreign silver coins changed hands in day-to-day transactions in colonial times.

Silver coins of various countries, notably the Spanish-American entities to the south such as Mexico, Chile, Peru, and others, remained legal tender in the United States until the Act of February 21, 1857, which provided for a two-year period for them to be exchanged for U.S. coins. (This was later given a six-month extension.) Foreign coins were used in domestic commerce for such a long period because there were insufficient U.S. coins in circulation.

The Philadelphia Mint, established in 1792, minted copper coins for circulation in 1793, but it was not until 1794 that its first silver issues were produced. (Surety bonds were required of Mint officials to permit precious metals to be handled, and it took some time for the bonds to be satisfied.) In autumn 1794 the first silver dollars were issued, in the amount of 1,758 pieces. In time, other silver denominations included the three-cent piece minted from 1851 to 1863, the half dime from 1794 to 1873, and the dime, quarter, and half dollar. (The latter three denominations are still produced for circulation today, but after 1964 they were no longer made of 90% silver, the standard alloy.)

With a small mintage of only 1,758 pieces, the 1794 silver dollar is rare in any condition. Even a worn example like this one—with its rough, scratched surfaces and damaged rims—can fetch a high price. It sold for $97,750 in an October 2008 auction.

Silver dollars were minted until 1935, after which "clad" (copper-nickel) dollars replaced them—the Eisenhower type starting in 1971 and the Susan B. Anthony in 1979. The Sacagawea dollar was introduced in 2000 in a "golden" alloy, with other Native American designs starting in 2009. Presidential dollars have been minted since 2007 in the same golden alloy (which doesn't actually contain gold). From 1875 to 1878 the shortest-lived of all American denominations, the silver twenty-cent piece, was minted. The silver trade dollar, intended for shipment to the Orient, was struck from 1873 to 1878. In addition, various commemorative coins and collectors' pieces have been made in silver. The metal has long been a numismatic favorite, and silver coins of all kinds are eagerly sought by collectors today.

"Five Silver Dollars Payable to the Bearer on Demand"—that's the guarantee on this Series of 1899 Silver Certificate. Which would you prefer: five one-dollar coins made of good old-fashioned American silver, or a piece of paper? For many years, most Americans preferred the hard metal, when they could get it.

SILVER CREATES EXCITEMENT WITH INVESTORS

Silver metal has been a popular investment for a long time. In the United States, coins of silver in the 18th and 19th centuries were always felt to be safer to hold than paper money, the latter being of uncertain value. Citizens of India and China vastly preferred silver to any other metals, including gold. From the 1500s onward, silver in coin form was a store of value for citizens, businesses, governments, and even pirates.

In America in the early 1900s there was not a great amount of popular interest in investing in silver. It was viewed mostly as a metal necessary in photographic film and, more visibly, for use in jewelry and ornamental goods. Sterling silver, an alloy of 92.5% silver plus 7.5% copper to add strength, was the standard. Items were simply marked STERLING to indicate this. In addition, silver-plated wares were popular.

The official price for silver, set by the government, was $1.2727 per ounce. The metal could be bought or sold at that price in virtually unlimited quantities. When in 1934 the price of gold was raised from $20.67 per

ounce to $35, silver remained at $1.2727. There the price stayed until the early 1960s, when demand for silver caused pressure on the market price. The value increased, and after 1964 it cost the U.S. Mint more than face value to make dimes, quarters, and half dollars—these being the silver denominations then produced. New copper-nickel-clad metal compositions took the place of standard .900 fine silver in 1965.

The first Kennedy half dollars, dated 1964, were coined in .900 fine silver. From 1965 to 1970, the coins were made in an alloy of net .400 fine silver. Since 1971, except for some Proofs struck for collectors, the half dollar has been made of copper-nickel, with no silver.

After 1964 the price of silver continued to rise. Any silver coins found in circulation were worth more than face value—and therefore profitable to remove from circulation and melt down. Great investment interest arose in bulk silver coins, while another market existed in ordinary Silver Certificates—the paper notes still in circulation, which could be exchanged for their equivalent in silver metal at the Treasury Department. A large business arose in this, many bankers and others who handled quantities of silver coins and paper bills made a lot of money, and one particular dealer even bought an airplane (a used DC-3) to go here and there to pick up quantities of certificates.

Interest in silver continued, and the Franklin Mint, a company whose stock was the #1 performer on the New York Stock Exchange for one year, did a great business in striking and selling millions of silver medals. At the same time there was a large and growing interest in "art bars" and "rounds," these being ingots or medals, generally made of an ounce of silver and bearing different artistic designs.

Bags of silver coins dated 1964 and earlier became a trading commodity, with bid and ask prices posted in *The Coin Dealer Newsletter* and elsewhere. In 1967, official trading of silver dollars as a security commenced.

The Franklin Mint struck millions of silver medals from the 1960s to the early 1980s. "By 1968 it was the Franklin Mint, not the Treasury, that had lines of collectors stretching down the block to acquire its products," writes Katherine Jaeger in the *Guide Book of United States Tokens and Medals*. "Its plant occupied 13 buildings, with 900 employees." Hiring many of the best artists of the day, by 1973 the company employed 19 sculptors who worked full time on dozens of medal series.

From a news release issued by the New York Mercantile Exchange, August 1, 1967 (with several numismatic errors corrected):

Spot Trading in Silver Dollars to Start August 21 on N.Y.M.E.

New York, N.Y.—Spot trading in silver dollars will start August 21, 1967, on the New York Mercantile Exchange, it was announced today. There will be two separate contracts, one calling for the delivery of used coins. Both contracts will permit delivery of either 'Peace' or 'Morgan' silver dollars of 'common date' years. The contracts both call for the delivery of 1,000 coins loose in a single canvas money bag of the type used by the United States Mint.

Common date silver dollars are from the years when the most coins were minted. Other silver dollars are of greater value than common date coins and thus would not logically be delivered. The value of these rarer silver dollars varies according to the year and the mint where they were struck. Morgan dollars were minted from 1878 to 1921 and 'Peace' dollars from 1921 to 1928 and 1934 to 1935. No silver dollars have been minted since 1935.

Trading hours for spot trading of silver dollars will be 12:00 noon to 2:00 p.m. Price changes will be in units of five dollars and prices will be posted to the nearest five dollars.

A spot check of coin dealers in the New York area this week shows 'common date' silver dollars at retail cost $1.75 used and $2.50 Uncirculated. It is estimated that about 847,000,000 silver dollars of the two varieties were minted in total and that a minimum of 330,000,000 were melted down by the government for the silver or for recasting. The number in existence is unknown. The government has on hand a total of only 3,000,000, all of rare dates and high numismatic value.

The *Wall Street Journal* and other financial publications took increased notice. Silver became hot, hot, hot! The *New York Times*, August 22, 1967, included this article on the same subject:

Commodity Men Watch Turnover in Silver Cartwheels.
"New 1880-S $1,000.: This was the stamping on a

white canvas bag out of which coin dealer Charles Ross spilled yesterday a shining flood of silver dollars atop a desk on the trading floor at the New York Mercantile Exchange. The time was 11:50 A.M. and in just 10 minutes trading was scheduled to begin in silver dollars. "The bag weighs about 60 pounds,: he explained to about two dozen brokers and clerks gathered around. "To be more exact, 59 pounds and 4 ounces for 1,000 coins. They are Uncirculated ones that came right out of the machines at the San Francisco Mint back in 1880." The small letter "S" indicated the San Francisco Mint. He said the bag was a regulation Treasury bag turned inside out and then marked, since he had looked over the coins and counted them.

Promptly at noon, Mr. Ross and other traders gathered around a board at the side of the trading floor, and the shouted bids and offers began. The pace was almost too fast for the three board members to chalk on blackboards the current prices and the initials of those who bid or offered them. Five new traders, all coin dealers, have joined the exchange, and the other members also can participate in the trading. Membership totals about 401, but only about 100 show up regularly to trade.

"There's going to be a lot of confusion," said one veteran floor trader. "I'm going back to potatoes." He darted toward the ring on the far side of the room where the exchange's main business—potato futures—takes place.

Amid the shouting it soon became evident that the prices of silver dollars were higher than many observers had expected. At the opening, a bag of Uncirculated coins sold at $2,300. Only five months ago, such a bag brought a price of $1,550, but that was before that talk about the silver shortage and the government's move to alleviate the *situation by auctioning silver to industrial users at prices above the $1.29 an ounce, where it had been pegged for many years.*

Yesterday's price of $2,300 brought a pleased smile from Darrell M. Hills, 33 years old, of Topeka, Kan., for whom the opening sale was made by his broker, "If the price was under $2,000 I planned to buy. If it was over $2,100 I planned to sell," Mr. Hills said. He is president of the Commodity Exchange Bulletin, an advisory service, and flew here primarily for the opening of trading.

Mr. Hills became interested in silver coins 10 years ago when he started a collection for his children. "The value seemed to grow each year. I've got about a 50 percent profit on the bag that sold at $2,300," he said.

Yesterday's prices surprised quite a few conservative commodity men because the underlying value at current price levels for silver is about $1.40 a coin. However, the coins retail in coin shops for anywhere from $1.75 to $2.50, depending on whether they are Uncirculated or whether they bear the obvious look of the wear-and-tear of having been in circulation. The exchange trades both types—circulated and Uncirculated.

At the close yesterday, the Uncirculated dollars, which opened at $2,300 a bag, sold as low as $2,200 and as high as $2,500. [Trading volume] totaled 32 bags. . . .

The die was cast—silver jumped into the mainstream of Wall Street investment, and attention increased as the years rolled on. Then, in the late 1970s, brothers Nelson Bunker Hunt and Herbert Hunt, Texas oil billionaires, launched an effort to corner the market in silver. At the time the metal was trading for about $6 per ounce. The Hunt brothers purchased raw metal and investment contracts in the commodity market, and in other ways laid claim to what some estimated as being one third of the world's floating supply of silver. Excitement spread, and American citizens rushed to take coins, tableware, jewelry, and other silver to dealers to turn it into cash. Entrepreneurs set up buying depots, and every coin shop had scales and coin-counting machines to accommodate the influx. At coin conventions there was a steady clinking and whir of machines on the trading floor as people arrived with their treasures.

In early January 1980 the price peaked at $48.70 per ounce, an all-time record. On January 7, new commodity-exchange rules were put into effect. Then the price began to fall. The Hunt brothers had purchased large amounts of the metal on margin and received calls for payment. These could not be met, and the market was thrown into a panic—the price of silver dropped 50% in four trading days. Thus began a long decline into the turn of the 21st century, with silver once again trading at $6 or less, and not much investor interest. Collectible medals were no longer in the news, the Franklin Mint had gone through ownership changes and was no longer prominent in the field, and ingots and art bars were history, with some minor exceptions.

In 1986 Uncle Sam got into the bullion game, and with a flourish. American Silver Eagles, as they are called, containing one ounce of silver, were launched, priced at bullion plus a premium. For an additional cost Proof strikings were made available to collectors. The bullion coins were instantly popular with investors and collectors alike.

The U.S. Mint's American Silver Eagle has proven to be a popular investment vehicle. "The obverse has Adolph A. Weinman's Liberty Walking design used on the half dollar coins from 1916 through 1947," notes the *Guide Book of United States Coins*. "The reverse design is a rendition of a heraldic eagle by John Mercanti."

In 2009 and 2010 silver was back in the spotlight with investors. Traders, investors, newsletter writers, and others followed the run-up in the price of *gold* and suggested that silver would rise sharply as well, as it had

The Challenge of Silver Production Statistics

I n the 19th century, when silver was front-row-center in politics, many attempts were made to estimate the historical production of that metal in America and the world. However, historical production statistics differ widely. Examples of this are provided by J. Laurence Laughlin, PhD, in *The History of Bimetallism in the United States*, 1900. The author quotes figures, no two of which are the same, from a variety of economic sources.

Taking as an example silver production in the world in the year 1868, Laughlin quoted Dr. Adolf Soetbeer's figure of $60,250,000; $50,000,000 from *Journal des Économistes*, March 1876; Sir Hector Hay's figure of $50,225,000; Ernest Seyd's similar figure of $50,225,000, Horton's figure of $46,750,000; and the U.S. Bureau of Statistics at $69,300,000.

You might assume the Bureau of Statistics' precise-sounding figure was correct — never mind that other sources, equally worthy of quoting, ranged as much as $22 million lower. Throughout 19th-century economics, precise-appearing figures give the feeling of numerical confidence not merited by the facts. The more you investigate the sources of such figures, the lower your confidence in them becomes. Even if economics later developed into a science, in the 1800s the discipline was much disorganized.

A similar situation arises when you try to determine the historical ratio of the value of gold to silver. Different economists have come up with different numbers. For example, for the year 1794, when dollars were first coined in the United States, Soetbeer quotes a ratio of 1 to 15.37, while White suggests 1 to 15.18, and Executive Document 117 of the First Session, 21st Congress, gives a ratio of 1 to 15.32. Each figure appears to be meticulously calculated. While these ratios are fairly close, for the year 1812 the respective figures from these three sources vary considerably and are for silver 16.11, 14.09, and 15.04 to 1.

Similarly, the *Annual Report of the Director of the Mint* for various years quotes average annual silver prices to three or even five decimal points, a precision not backed up by actual market numbers, which were much less precise. Such "precision" arose from adding up hundreds of market figures for a given year and then dividing by the time interval involved.

The averaging of many numbers could and did produce statistics of unintended precision — just as 2/3 or two-thirds, a proportion expressed casually, does not necessarily imply a precision of 0.6666666666+.

Today, the annual production of silver is not known in precise terms. Guesses and estimates abound. A typical figure is 500 million ounces per year, with investment gurus stating this is insufficient for demand, which is said to be several hundred million ounces more than that. The demand for silver in commerce, such as for electrical goods, jewelry, commemorative coins and medals, medicine, and the like holds fairly steady, while the demand by investors is largely based on psychology.

done in the late 1970s. This came true; by autumn 2010 the price was over $25 per ounce, and that winter it reached $30. Predictions attract a lot of attention when made, but are forgotten if they don't pan out. Accordingly, predictions of $100 per ounce or more for silver and $5,000 for gold were not unusual. At this time many commodities were rising in price across the board, including copper and other non-precious metals, fueled by industrial demand from China, hedging elsewhere, and a worldwide philosophy that metals were a safety net amid turmoil in certain currency markets.

In 2011 silver is very much in the spotlight, with many traders continuing to publish optimistic reports. Investors would do well to be cautious, and if silver in the form of bullion or bulk coins is purchased, to actually take physical possession of it, rather than being satisfied with paper certificates or guarantees.

Silver has long been used in coinage and to commemorate people, places, and events (as illustrated by these American and European medals). However, only in recent decades has the precious metal been actively pursued as an investment.

PLATINUM
9995

1 OUNCE TROY

3

THE PLATINUM GROUP

In 1997 the U.S. Mint began producing platinum coins, called *eagles* (the same name used for silver and gold bullion issues), for precious-metal investors and numismatists. There was no history of this rare metal being used for circulating coinage in America, although in the early 1800s (when platinum was a newly discovered metal) several pattern or test pieces were struck by the Mint.

United States Pattern Coins, 10th edition, notes that "The circumstances of the production of the platinum 1814 half dollars are not known. . . . [It] is one of only a few original early 19th-century United States pattern coin varieties in existence today." Only three specimens are thought to exist; if a fourth is discovered, it might be worth $100,000 or more.

Russia issued platinum coins for circulation in the early 1800s. This 1829 three-ruble coin was one of a mintage of 343,000.

The 1997 coinage was denominated in values of $10, $25, $50, and $100, containing one-tenth, one-quarter, one-half, and one ounce respectively of pure platinum. Coins sold singly and in sets have been produced since that time, each with designs not used elsewhere in the American series.

Common Obverse for Proof Platinum Coinage

1998: "Eagle Over New England"

1999: "Eagle Above Southeastern Wetlands"

2000: "Eagle Above America's Heartland"

2001: "Eagle Above America's Southwest"

2002: "Eagle Fishing in America's Northwest"

The U.S. Mint's platinum bullion-coin motifs of 1998 to 2002, showing eagles flying through various American scenes, are known collectively as the "Vistas of Liberty." (shown 1.5x actual size)

Since 2003 they have featured patriotic allegories and symbolism. From 2006 to 2008 the reverse designs honored "The Foundations of Democracy"—the nation's legislative branch (2006), executive branch (2007), and judicial branch (2008). In 2009 the Mint introduced a new six-year program of reverse designs, exploring the core concepts of American democracy as embodied in the preamble to the Constitution. The first design is *To Form a More Perfect Union* (2009), featuring four faces representing the nation's diversity, with the hair and clothing interweaving symbolically. The tiny eagle privy mark is from an original coin punch from the Philadelphia Mint's archives. This design is followed by *To Establish Justice* (2010), *To Insure Domestic Tranquility* (2011), *To Provide for the Common Defence* (2012), *To Promote the General Welfare* (2013), and

2003

2004: "America," after Daniel Chester French

2005

2006: "Legislative Branch"

2007: "Executive Branch"

2008: "Judicial Branch"

2009: "To Form a More Perfect Union"

2010: "To Establish Justice"

The U.S. Mint's platinum bullion-coin motifs of 2003 through 2010. (shown 1.5x actual size)

To Secure the Blessings of Liberty to Ourselves and our Posterity (2014). The themes for the reverse designs are inspired by narratives prepared by the chief justice of the United States.

When it comes to coins struck for circulation (as opposed to patterns, commemoratives, or bullion), the first and only use of platinum took place in Russia beginning in 1828 and continuing intermittently to 1845. The coinage proved to be impractical, as the metal was difficult to strike (due to its hardness) and, perhaps more importantly, there was no way that citizens could differentiate platinum from silver. In the late 1820s the Royal Mint in London prepared some pattern coins in this metal, but nothing came of the venture.

A renewed interest in platinum for commemorative and bullion coinage began in the Soviet Union in 1978, and later in Australia, Canada, China, and the Isle of Man. Countries that have issued platinum coins in recent years include Congo, Estonia, France, Great Britain, Monaco, Panama, Portugal, South Africa, Switzerland, and Tonga, among others. Such programs had limited popularity for a time, but after 2005 the United States was the only country actively making platinum coins.

This French platinum coin celebrates the centennial of the Statue of Liberty—the monument was a gift from the people of France to the United States in 1886. Platinum commemorative coins often have small mintages. Only 9,500 of these 100-franc pieces were struck.

In 2006 this British platinum coin trumpeted the 80th birthday of Queen Elizabeth II. Only 250 pieces were issued.

This platinum coin of Bhutan celebrated the accession of King Jigme Dorji Wangchuck. A mere 72 pieces were minted. The coin sold at auction in January 2011 for $3,450.

This Swiss "shooting thaler"— an ounce of platinum—shows William Tell and his son.

The 1988 Olympics in Seoul were the subject of this half-ounce platinum commemorative from Tonga.

Platinum is the most important metal in the so-called platinum group, which comprises indium, osmium, palladium, platinum, rhodium, and ruthenium, each of which is rare as a commodity. Except for platinum (and palladium beginning in the United States in 2011), none has been used for coinage.

Obverse   Reverse

Designs of Uncirculated U.S. platinum bullion coinage.

The melting point of platinum is 3,214.97 degrees Fahrenheit, and its density is 19.77 grams per cubic centimeter. Most platinum is obtained as a byproduct of the processing of nickel and copper ore. In 2006, an estimated 239 tons of platinum were sold, with 130 tons used in vehicle emission-control devices, 49 for jewelry, 13.3 for electronics, and 11.2 in the chemical industry. Electrodes, wires, electrical contacts, and thermocouples use platinum, as do certain medical devices and dental prostheses. The metal does not corrode, making it useful for specialized applications. Similar to palladium, the surface will develop a surface haze over time.

In recent decades the use of platinum in jewelry has been emphasized, while at the same time the word *platinum* has been promoted as an adjective above that of gold—for example, an American Express Platinum Card costs more and gives more benefits than a Gold Card. Historically, typical competitive rankings had been gold, then silver, then bronze. (In some fields, such as the issuance of record albums, "diamond" trumps platinum. A release selling more than a million copies is called platinum and one selling more than 10 million is referred to as diamond.)

Platinum is an ideal setting for a diamond, such as this 3.37-carat center stone flanked by two tapered baguette accents.

Platinum is not a monetary metal in the sense that gold is. It has, however, drawn great interest among speculators. These factors have combined to make its value volatile in recent years. In 2008 the price per ounce ranged from $774 to $2,252. A popular way for promoters to

Australia's platinum koalas were made for collectors and bullion investors.

encourage investment sales of platinum, gold, and silver is to take the current market price and predict that in the near future the value will increase dramatically—and "now is the time to lock in your investment."

The first and only bimetallic issue in the U.S. commemorative series is this 2000 coin honoring the bicentennial of the Library of Congress. A ring of gold surrounds a central planchet of platinum. This commemorative was ranked no. 25 among the *100 Greatest U.S. Modern Coins*, in the book of the same name.

PALLADIUM: A RELATIVE NEWCOMER

In 2011 the U.S. Mint is slated to use the rare metal palladium for coinage for the first time. This follows several years of legislative maneuvering that resulted in the American Eagle Palladium Bullion Act of 2010, which passed the House of Representatives on September 22, 2010, and the Senate on September 28, and was signed into law by President Barack Obama on November 30. The act specifies that the coins are to contain one ounce of .9995 fine palladium and to bear the denomination of twenty-five dollars.

Although the U.S. Mint today has more sculptor-engravers and consulting artists than at any other time in its history, it was decided to resurrect old designs for the new palladium coins. For the obverse, Adolph A. Weinman's "Winged Liberty Head" or "Mercury" motif was selected. This is the design originally used on dimes from 1916 to 1947. For the reverse an obscure image was chosen: that created by Weinman for the 1907 American Institute of Architects medal.

The lustrous silver-white metal has never been used for circulating coins anywhere in the world. The 2011 appearance of palladium bul-

The U.S. Mint's new palladium bullion coins will look something like this old Mercury dime.

lion coinage is intended to provide an investment vehicle for precious-metal investors.

Palladium is a member of the platinum group of metals, which share similar chemical properties. Discovered in 1803 by William Hyde Wolliston, it has the chemical symbol Pd and has the lowest melting point (2,830.82 degrees Fahrenheit) and is the least dense metal (12.023 grams per cubic centimeter) in its group.

The maiden voyage of the RMS *Queen Elizabeth 2* was celebrated with a privately issued palladium medal (shown here at half of its actual 65 mm diameter).

This Bermuda coin shows a scene of the shipwreck of the *San Antonio*. Only 2,000 pieces were minted. The one-ounce palladium coin sold at auction in early 2009 for $230—about the bullion value of the metal itself. Two years later, that value had tripled.

Czar Peter the Great stares imperiously from this 25-ruble Soviet commemorative honoring the 500th year of the Russian state. The coin was struck in palladium in 1990.

In industry platinum finds use in electrical contacts and components in catalytic convertors (its main market), ceramic capacitors, cell phones, and computers, among other products. It is also used in dentistry, medicine, and fuel cells, and in the purification of hydrogen gas and ground water. As a precious metal palladium has been used in jewelry since about 1939, as an inexpensive alternative to platinum and as a component of white gold. Similar to gold, it is very malleable and ductile and can be beaten into thin sheets. A drawback to its use in jewelry is that it cannot be readily distinguished by eye as a precious metal, and it tends to develop a hazy surface over time (as does platinum). Preventing or slowing the development of this haze on the new U.S. bullion coins may be a challenge.

The legislation enabling the palladium coinage specified that the metal must have been extracted within the past year from a Montana deposit (the only commercially feasible one in the United States), from the Stillwater Igneous Complex, a large layered intrusion of ore visible across 30 miles of the north flank of the Beartooth Mountain Range. To view it objectively, the legislation was a prize to the Montana industry, similar to the Bland-Allison Act of February 28, 1878, which mandated that Uncle Sam buy large quantities of silver, to support the Western silver-mining industry.

Palladium was a popular term in the 19th century for a number of things other than the metal. For example, in Massachusetts, *Worcester Palladium* was a popular newspaper. Palladium was also used for dance halls and the like, in America and in Europe—the famous London Palladium being an example. Palladium deposits exist in the Transvaal Basin in South Africa, the Norilsk Complex in Russia, and the Sudbury District of Ontario, Canada. In 2005 the estimated worldwide demand for the metal was about 1.4 million ounces.

This Proof palladium commemorative from Bermuda celebrates the *Sea Venture*—a 17th-century English sailing ship whose wreck may have inspired Shakespeare's *The Tempest*.

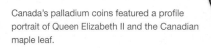

Canada's palladium coins featured a profile portrait of Queen Elizabeth II and the Canadian maple leaf.

THE PRICES OF PLATINUM AND PALLADIUM, PER OUNCE

Annual Averages (London Market Price), 1992–2011

Year	Platinum	Palladium	Year	Platinum	Palladium
1992	$360.92	$89.03	2002	$539.13	$337.57
1993	$374.14	$122.35	2003	$691.31	$200.27
1994	$404.95	$142.61	2004	$845.31	$229.37
1995	$424.38	$151.26	2005	$896.87	$201.37
1996	$397.12	$128.06	2006	$1,142.31	$320.27
1997	$395.23	$178.04	2007	$1,303.05	$354.86
1998	$372.15	$284.83	2008	$1,573.53	$351.51
1999	$377.93	$358.02	2009	$1,203.49	$263.27
2000	$544.03	$680.79	2010	$1,608.98	$525.51
2001	$529.04	$603.86	2011	~$1,800.00	~$780.00

These graceful ballerinas danced on commemorative palladium coins of the Soviet Union in 1990.

The Isle of Man issued a palladium coin marking the 200th anniversary of the discovery of the metal itself.

Early 1980: people line up outside a coin shop in Louisville, Kentucky, eager to sell their gold for record prices. Ten years earlier, gold was worth about $36 an ounce. That January it peaked at $850.

THE RECENT PRECIOUS METALS BOOM

On January 21, 1980, gold bullion peaked at the then-astounding price of $850 per ounce—incredible compared to its value of about $175 two years earlier. This was against the backdrop of unprecedented inflation and an attempt by the Hunt brothers and other investors to corner the silver market. The Dow Jones Industrial Average was also around $850 in 1980.

Two decades later the Dow surged past $10,000 and gold was considered a relic of the financial world, having slipped to only $250 per ounce by September of 1999. For much of the next ten years gold was ignored by most investors.

Positive wealth effect: An increase in wealth that results in a rise in consumption and thus an increase in production and employment.

Everything seemed great with the U.S. economy for most of the 2000s. Anyone with a pulse could buy a house. Interest rates were at historic lows, and refinancing was all the rage. The positive wealth effect had taken hold in America. Everyone had money (or had access to it), and spending on cars, boats, and luxury goods soared. The bubble finally burst, however, in the fall of 2008. Home prices began to ratchet down, and a financial term most had never heard of—the CDO, or collateralized debt obligation—made headlines. Banks and other institutions were on the hook for trillions of dollars in potentially bad loans. The American auto industry was also on the ropes and facing dire consequences.

THE PRICE OF GOLD PER OUNCE, 1933–2009

Governments kept the value of gold steady for centuries. This chart shows how the value has risen in recent years.

Year	New York Market Price	Year	New York Market Price	Year	New York Market Price
1933	$24.44	1951	$35.00	1969	$41.51
1934	$34.94	1952	$35.00	1970	$36.41
1935	$35.00	1953	$35.00	1971	$41.25
1936	$35.00	1954	$35.00	1972	$58.60
1937	$35.00	1955	$35.00	1973	$97.81
1938	$35.00	1956	$35.00	1974	$159.74
1939	$35.00	1957	$35.00	1975	$161.49
1940	$35.00	1958	$35.00	1976	$125.32
1941	$35.00	1959	$35.00	1977	$148.31
1942	$35.00	1960	$35.00	1978	$193.55
1943	$35.00	1961	$35.00	1979	$307.50
1944	$35.00	1962	$35.00	1980	$612.56
1945	$35.00	1963	$35.00	1981	$459.64
1946	$35.00	1964	$35.00	1982	$375.91
1947	$35.00	1965	$35.00	1983	$424.00
1948	$35.00	1966	$35.00	1984	$360.66
1949	$35.00	1967	$35.00	1985	$317.66
1950	$35.00	1968	$39.26	1986	$368.24

Year	New York Market Price	Year	New York Market Price	Year	New York Market Price
1987	$447.95	1995	$385.50	2003	$364.80
1988	$438.31	1996	$389.09	2004	$410.52
1989	$382.58	1997	$332.39	2005	$446.00
1990	$384.93	1998	$295.24	2006	$606.00
1991	$363.29	1999	$279.91	2007	$699.00
1992	$344.97	2000	$280.10	2008	$900.00
1993	$360.91	2001	$272.22	2009	$910.00
1994	$385.42	2002	$311.33	2010	$1,124.53

1933–2008 data courtesy of MeasuringWorth (www.measuringworth.org).

Soon global markets were on the brink of collapse. The United States and the rest of the world were facing the very real possibility of a second "Great Depression." Several household-name financial institutions such as Lehman Brothers were closing their doors for good. Fannie Mae, Freddie Mac, AIG, and Citigroup were saved only by massive government intervention. (Today, after federal bailouts, these companies are basically government entities. The Royal Bank of Scotland, at one time the world's largest bank, is also under governmental control, in Britain.) The Dow Jones Industrial Average dropped from a peak of around $14,000 to below $7,000. Retirement accounts of nearly every American have plunged in value. For the first time in decades there has been a huge *negative* wealth effect gripping the country.

As the U.S. economy sank in 2008 and 2009, people began to make comparisons to the Great Depression—and some predicted a repeat of history. In times of war, inflation, and other national challenges, more and more people see gold and silver as security. This photograph of a destitute pea picker and her children is from early 1936; in it, photographer Dorothea Lange captured the Depression era's sadness and worry. . . emotions not unknown in today's trying times.

Most experts agree that governments around the globe needed to act fast to head off a meltdown of the financial system and to protect capitalism as we knew it. The U.S. government instituted several creative yet expensive programs to deal with the crisis. One of the largest was the $700 billion TARP (Toxic Asset Relief Program), created to purchase or insure troubled assets from banks and other financial institutions. There was also Cash for Clunkers; an $8,000 first-time homebuyer tax credit; and large investments in the automotive sector. In addition to these expensive programs, the nation was at war on two fronts, with a cost of more than $11 billion per month.

The Stimulus Effect on Precious Metals

The stock markets have reacted positively to the massive government stimulus programs. By late 2009 the Dow sat above the $10,000 level for the first time in several months. The housing market seems to have finally bottomed out and stopped falling. Banks are now recording large profits. Unemployment, however, has stayed around the 10% level, and there is already talk of further federal stimulus spending in the works.

In light of this massive spending it is no surprise that the federal deficit has ballooned more than $1.5 trillion since early 2009. A larger and larger share of individual income taxes will be used to make interest payments on a federal debt that now totals a staggering $14 trillion and counting. The strength of the American dollar has fallen as confidence in our currency wanes. By nearly every estimate given by experts, pundits, and governmental agencies, the deficit spending will continue for the foreseeable future.

As would be expected, tangible assets have become quite popular. In less than six years gold has risen from $450 per ounce to around $1,400, and silver from about $5 to near $30. The demand is global, as governments and individuals seek the safety of precious metals. Investors today are very much interested in protecting wealth and hav-

Gold comes in many forms: bars, coins, flakes, nuggets . . . all valuable, all eagerly sought by investors and collectors. These are from the ship-wreck of the SS *Central America,* lost at sea in a hurricane in 1857.

ing a hedge against the possibility of massive inflation. There is a growing sense in the United States and around the world that our federal deficit is out of control. For more than 2,000 years gold in particular has been a store of value, and until the last century closely tied to the value of our currency. Many investors now believe it is vital to have gold and silver as part of any portfolio. What once seemed to be obsolete investment vehicles are now two of the most widely discussed subjects in financial circles.

Precious metals are among the hottest topics on CNBC, Fox Financial News, and Bloomberg. The airwaves are full of ads selling gold and silver for investment and seeking to buy your unwanted scrap. Gold even made the 2009 Super Bowl, when a company ran a halftime commercial starring Ed McMahon and MC Hammer—at a cost of more than $2 million.

This onslaught of advertising can be quite confusing. The purpose of this book is to provide you with information and tools to make smart moves when buying or selling precious metals. They can be very exciting to purchase, but it is extremely important to do your homework when spending hard-earned money on any investment. Similarly, education is your key when it's time to sell. After reading this book, you will have a great head start in making the right decisions.

CHAPTER

SELLING YOUR PRECIOUS METALS

With the recent increase in bullion prices, many investors are using this opportunity to take profits or raise capital. Many long-term gold and silver bulls have anxiously waited for the day that their predictions of inflation or financial calamity would lead to a jump in precious-metal prices. Other people, however, have become strapped for cash as unemployment surges and the economy weakens during a prolonged recession. A 2010 study published in *USA Today* stated that 40% of the U.S. population had no "rainy day" fund and 20% had borrowed money in the last year from payday lenders or pawn shops.

SELLING SCRAP PRECIOUS METALS

Gold is one of the rarest metals on earth. It is estimated that only 125,000 tons of gold have been mined in the last 5,000 years. Silver, while also scarce, was mined worldwide to the tune of some 30,000 tons in 2007 alone.

For hundreds of years gold and silver have been stores of wealth in times of crisis. Today there are reports from around the country of individuals selling old jewelry to make ends meet. Unfortunately, many have no idea of how to value the metal they are attempting to sell.

A quick search on Google found more than a million results for "scrap gold buyers." It seems everyone wants to buy your old gold and silver. Most local newspapers have at least one full-page ad every week from firms claiming to be the high buyer. Radio, TV, and the Internet are full of ads,

When times are tough, scrap gold and silver come out of hiding to make ends meet.

as well. It seems we have entered a modern-day "Gold and Silver Rush." The ads make it all sound so simple—drop your precious metal in the mail and a few days later, money appears on your doorstep!

One of the first things to keep in mind when selling precious metals to a large advertiser is that you, the *seller*, are the one ultimately paying for the advertising blitz. Advertising is very expensive, and you can be certain the price you receive reflects the cost of attracting your business. The best protection for sellers is to know the facts about what you are attempting to sell. Blindly accepting an offer when you have no clue of the true value is a poor idea. The range of offers from buyers of scrap gold, for example, can vary from 90% of true spot gold value down to a mere 10%. You owe it to yourself to understand how this market works.

FINENESS OF GOLD AND SILVER

For centuries the purity of gold has been measured in karats (1 karat being 1/24 fine gold by weight). Pure gold is 24 karat (24k). Gold and silver are sometimes described by their fineness, which is the purity per 1,000 parts in a given mass. For example, 900 fine gold is an alloy of 90% pure gold with 10% other metals added. Federal Trade Commission rules require all gold jewelry sold in the United States to be marked with "correct designation of the karat fineness of the alloy." An item that appears to be gold but is unmarked for fineness often is only gold-filled or gold-plated. Gold test kits can be found easily on the Internet or at some jewelry stores. Coin silver was typically 90% pure, with copper added for strength. Sterling silver, by definition, is 925 parts fine.

Americans aren't the only ones fascinated by gold and silver. An old tobacco-advertising card illustrates Australia's fabled "Welcome Nugget" of gold—weighing 2,217 ounces and "exceeding in purity and value any lump of gold ever found." Discovered in 1858 and later exhibited at the Crystal Palace in London, the Welcome Nugget was eventually melted down and struck into gold sovereigns.

WEIGHING SCRAP PRECIOUS METALS

The weight of a piece of jewelry is a main factor when determining its melt value. The gram (g) and the pennyweight (dwt) are the units most commonly used in weighing gold. Gold and silver are usually weighed in the troy system of weights, where

> 1 pound troy = 12 troy ounces, and
> 20 pennyweights = 1 troy ounce.

The troy ounce is the traditional unit of weight for precious metals such as gold and silver (as well as for gems and sometimes pharmaceuticals). Troy comes from the French town of Troyes, where the measurement unit was first used, in medieval times. One troy ounce is slightly more than one avoirdupois ounce (avoirdupois is the system used to weigh other goods). In the troy system, there are 12 ounces to a pound; in avoirdupois, there are 16. When gold and silver are involved, typically any reference to an ounce *means a troy ounce.*

WEIGHT CONVERSION TABLES

1 gram (g)	0.643 dwt
1 pennyweight (dwt)	1.555 g
1 troy ounce (oz t)	31.103 g

Karat Gold	Parts Gold	Percentage Gold
9k	9 in 24	37.50%
10 kt	10 in 24	41.67%
12 kt	12 in 24	50.00%
14 kt	14 in 24	58.33%
18 kt	18 in 24	75.00%
22 kt	22 in 24	91.67%
24 kt	24 in 24	99.99%

CALCULATING MELT VALUE OF SCRAP GOLD, PER PENNYWEIGHT

Karat	When gold is $900/ounce	When gold is $950/ounce	When gold is $1,000/ounce	When gold is $1,050/ounce	When gold is $1,100/ounce
9	$16.87	$17.81	$18.75	$19.68	$20.62
10	18.75	19.79	20.83	21.25	22.93
12	22.50	23.75	25.00	26.25	27.50
14	26.24	27.70	29.16	30.62	32.08
18	33.75	35.63	37.50	39.37	41.25
22	41.25	43.54	45.83	46.75	50.41
24	45.00	47.50	50.00	52.50	55.00

Karat	When gold is $1,150/ounce	When gold is $1,200/ounce	When gold is $1,250/ounce	When gold is $1,300/ounce	When gold is $1,350/ounce
9	$21.06	$22.50	$23.44	$24.38	$25.31
10	23.96	25.00	26.04	27.09	28.13
12	27.25	30.00	31.25	32.50	33.75
14	33.54	35.00	36.42	37.91	39.33
18	43.12	45.00	46.88	48.75	50.63
22	52.71	55.00	57.29	59.59	61.88
24	57.50	60.00	62.50	65.00	67.50

Karat	When gold is $1,400/ounce	When gold is $1,450/ounce	When gold is $1,500/ounce	When gold is $1,550/ounce
9	$26.25	$27.19	$28.13	$29.06
10	29.17	30.21	31.25	32.29
12	35.00	36.25	37.50	38.75
14	40.83	42.25	43.75	45.16
18	52.50	54.38	56.25	58.13
22	64.17	66.46	68.75	71.04
24	70.00	72.50	75.00	77.50

WEIGHT CONVERSION FOR GOLD: GRAMS TO PENNYWEIGHT

grams	dwt	grams	dwt	grams	dwt	grams	dwt
1	0.643	32	20.576	63	40.509	94	60.442
2	1.286	33	21.219	64	41.152	95	61.085
3	1.929	34	21.862	65	41.795	96	61.728
4	2.572	35	22.505	66	42.438	97	62.371
5	3.215	36	23.148	67	43.081	98	63.014
6	3.858	37	23.791	68	43.724	99	63.657
7	4.501	38	24.434	69	44.367	100	64.300
8	5.144	39	25.077	70	45.010	101	64.943
9	5.787	40	25.720	71	45.653	102	65.586
10	6.430	41	26.363	72	46.296	103	66.229
11	7.073	42	27.006	73	46.939	104	66.872
12	7.716	43	27.649	74	47.582	105	67.515
13	8.359	44	28.292	75	48.225	106	68.158
14	9.002	45	28.935	76	48.868	107	68.801
15	9.645	46	29.578	77	49.511	108	69.444
16	10.288	47	30.221	78	50.154	109	70.087
17	10.931	48	30.864	79	50.797	110	70.730
18	11.574	49	31.507	80	51.440	111	71.373
19	12.217	50	32.150	81	52.083	112	72.016
20	12.860	51	32.793	82	52.726	113	72.659
21	13.503	52	33.436	83	53.369	114	73.302
22	14.146	53	34.079	84	54.012	115	73.945
23	14.789	54	34.722	85	54.655	116	74.588
24	15.432	55	35.365	86	55.298	117	75.231
25	16.075	56	36.008	87	55.941	118	75.874
26	16.718	57	36.651	88	56.584	119	76.517
27	17.361	58	37.294	89	57.227	120	77.160
28	18.004	59	37.937	90	57.870	121	77.803
29	18.647	60	38.580	91	58.513	122	78.446
30	19.290	61	39.223	92	59.156	123	79.089
31	19.933	62	39.866	93	59.799	124	79.732

grams	dwt	grams	dwt	grams	dwt	grams	dwt
125	80.375	157	100.951	189	121.527	221	142.103
126	81.018	158	101.594	190	122.170	222	142.746
127	81.661	159	102.237	191	122.813	223	143.389
128	82.304	160	102.880	192	123.456	224	144.032
129	82.947	161	103.523	193	124.099	225	144.675
130	83.590	162	104.166	194	124.742	226	145.318
131	84.233	163	104.809	195	125.385	227	145.961
132	84.876	164	105.452	196	126.028	228	146.604
133	85.519	165	106.095	197	126.671	229	147.247
134	86.162	166	106.738	198	127.314	230	147.890
135	86.805	167	107.381	199	127.957	231	148.533
136	87.448	168	108.024	200	128.600	232	149.176
137	88.091	169	108.667	201	129.243	233	149.819
138	88.734	170	109.310	202	129.886	234	150.462
139	89.377	171	109.953	203	130.529	235	151.105
140	90.020	172	110.596	204	131.172	236	151.748
141	90.663	173	111.239	205	131.815	237	152.391
142	91.306	174	111.882	206	132.458	238	153.034
143	91.949	175	112.525	207	133.101	239	153.677
144	92.592	176	113.168	208	133.744	240	154.320
145	93.235	177	113.811	209	134.387	241	154.963
146	93.878	178	114.454	210	135.030	242	155.606
147	94.521	179	115.097	211	135.673	243	156.249
148	95.164	180	115.740	212	136.316	244	156.892
149	95.807	181	116.383	213	136.959	245	157.535
150	96.450	182	117.026	214	137.602	246	158.178
151	97.093	183	117.669	215	138.245	247	158.821
152	97.736	184	118.312	216	138.888	248	159.464
153	98.379	185	118.955	217	139.531	249	160.107
154	99.022	186	119.598	218	140.174	250	160.750
155	99.665	187	120.241	219	140.817		
156	100.308	188	120.884	220	141.460		

1 gram (g) = 0.643 pennyweight (dwt) • 1 pennyweight (dwt) = 1.555 g • 1 troy ounce (oz t) = 31.103 g

WEIGHT CONVERSION FOR GOLD: PENNYWEIGHT TO GRAMS

dwt	grams	dwt	grams	dwt	grams	dwt	grams
1	1.555	32	49.760	63	97.965	94	146.170
2	3.110	33	51.315	64	99.520	95	147.725
3	4.665	34	52.870	65	101.075	96	149.280
4	6.220	35	54.425	66	102.630	97	150.835
5	7.775	36	55.980	67	104.185	98	152.390
6	9.330	37	57.535	68	105.740	99	153.945
7	10.885	38	59.090	69	107.295	100	155.500
8	12.440	39	60.645	70	108.850	101	157.055
9	13.995	40	62.200	71	110.405	102	158.610
10	15.550	41	63.755	72	111.960	103	160.165
11	17.105	42	65.310	73	113.515	104	161.720
12	18.660	43	66.865	74	115.070	105	163.275
13	20.215	44	68.420	75	116.625	106	164.830
14	21.770	45	69.975	76	118.180	107	166.385
15	23.325	46	71.530	77	119.735	108	167.940
16	24.880	47	73.085	78	121.290	109	169.495
17	26.435	48	74.640	79	122.845	110	171.050
18	27.990	49	76.195	80	124.400	111	172.605
19	29.545	50	77.750	81	125.955	112	174.160
20	31.100	51	79.305	82	127.510	113	175.715
21	32.655	52	80.860	83	129.065	114	177.270
22	34.210	53	82.415	84	130.620	115	178.825
23	35.765	54	83.970	85	132.175	116	180.380
24	37.320	55	85.525	86	133.730	117	181.935
25	38.875	56	87.080	87	135.285	118	183.490
26	40.430	57	88.635	88	136.840	119	185.045
27	41.985	58	90.190	89	138.395	120	186.600
28	43.540	59	91.745	90	139.950	121	188.155
29	45.095	60	93.300	91	141.505	122	189.710
30	46.650	61	94.855	92	143.060	123	191.265
31	48.205	62	96.410	93	144.615	124	192.820

dwt	grams	dwt	grams	dwt	grams	dwt	grams
125	194.375	157	244.135	189	293.895	221	343.655
126	195.930	158	245.690	190	295.450	222	345.210
127	197.485	159	247.245	191	297.005	223	346.765
128	199.040	160	248.800	192	298.560	224	348.320
129	200.595	161	250.355	193	300.115	225	349.875
130	202.150	162	251.910	194	301.670	226	351.430
131	203.705	163	253.465	195	303.225	227	352.985
132	205.260	164	255.020	196	304.780	228	354.540
133	206.815	165	256.575	197	306.335	229	356.095
134	208.370	166	258.130	198	307.890	230	357.650
135	209.925	167	259.685	199	309.445	231	359.205
136	211.480	168	261.240	200	311.000	232	360.760
137	213.035	169	262.795	201	312.555	233	362.315
138	214.590	170	264.350	202	314.110	234	363.870
139	216.145	171	265.905	203	315.665	235	365.425
140	217.700	172	267.460	204	317.220	236	366.980
141	219.255	173	269.015	205	318.775	237	368.535
142	220.810	174	270.570	206	320.330	238	370.090
143	222.365	175	272.125	207	321.885	239	371.645
144	223.920	176	273.680	208	323.440	240	373.200
145	225.475	177	275.235	209	324.995	241	374.755
146	227.030	178	276.790	210	326.550	242	376.310
147	228.585	179	278.345	211	328.105	243	377.865
148	230.140	180	279.900	212	329.660	244	379.420
149	231.695	181	281.455	213	331.215	245	380.975
150	233.250	182	283.010	214	332.770	246	382.530
151	234.805	183	284.565	215	334.325	247	384.085
152	236.360	184	286.120	216	335.880	248	385.640
153	237.915	185	287.675	217	337.435	249	387.195
154	239.470	186	289.230	218	338.990	250	388.750
155	241.025	187	290.785	219	340.545		
156	242.580	188	292.340	220	342.100		

1 gram (g) = 0.643 pennyweight (dwt)   •   1 pennyweight (dwt) = 1.555 g   •   1 troy ounce (oz t) = 31.103 g

BUYING A SCALE

Checking the actual weight of your unwanted jewelry or scrap gold and silver is quite easy. Inexpensive electronic scales are available at many jewelry stores or on the Internet. Amazon.com and other online retailers offer several brands for around $20. This can be the best investment you make when considering the disposal of your precious metals. Check the weight and use the tables in this book to calculate the actual melt value of your holdings.

SELLING PRECIOUS-METAL BULLION

Bullion comes in many forms, the most commonly seen being bars and coins. There are hundreds of different gold and silver coins that commonly trade as bullion. Platinum and, especially, palladium are less common as bullion, but they do exist in bullion-coin form; see chapter 3. Many years ago, when gold was illegal to own in the United States, the South African Krugerrand was the favorite coin of most investors. Now many governments, including that of the United States, offer gold and silver bullion coins. The U.S. Mint sells millions of American Eagles each year in both metals.

The Mint also makes 24-karat (.9999 fine) "American Buffalo" gold bullion coins, and a variety of "First Spouse" gold coins.

American Silver Eagle bullion coins have a face value of $1—obviously, much lower than their actual precious-metal value, since each coin has an ounce of silver. The obverse recreates Adolph A. Weinman's Liberty Walking design from the half dollar of 1916 to 1947. The reverse features a heraldic eagle designed by John Mercanti. (Shown actual size)

American Eagle gold bullion coins are made in four denominations that contain from one-tenth ounce to one full ounce of .9167 fine gold. The obverse features a modified rendition of the Augustus Saint-Gaudens design used on U.S. $20 gold pieces from 1907 to 1933. The reverse displays a "family of eagles" motif.

Uncirculated American Eagle gold bullion coins are not sold directly to the general public, but to a series of authorized buyers. They obtain the coins from the Mint based on the current spot price plus a small premium. The coins are then sold to secondary distributors for sale to other dealers and to the public. The Mint does sell special collector versions of the coins (Proofs, and, starting in 2006, "burnished" specimens) directly to individual collectors. (All shown at 1.5x actual size)

American Buffalo gold bullion coins were the first .9999 fine (24-karat) gold coins made by the U.S. Mint. They are struck at the West Point facility and distributed in the same manner as American Eagle gold bullion coins. In 2006 and 2007, only one-ounce coins (with a $50 face value) were minted. Starting in 2008 the Mint also produced half-ounce ($25 face value), quarter-ounce ($10), and tenth-ounce ($5) pieces, in both Proof and Uncirculated formats, individually and in sets. As with other gold bullion coins, their values change frequently and are based on prevailing bullion and fabrication costs relative to the weight of each denomination. ($50 coin pictured; actual size 32.7 mm).

Jackson's Liberty

Julia Tyler

The U.S. Mint's First Spouse gold bullion coins (like the samples shown here) are struck in .9999 fine (24-karat) gold. They weigh one-half ounce and have a face value of $10—though of course they're worth much more for their gold content. The coins honor the nation's first ladies. Each features a portrait on the obverse, and on the reverse a unique design symbolic of her life and work. (Some coins don't have a portrait; in instances where a president held office without a spouse, the coin bears "an obverse image emblematic of Liberty as depicted on a circulating coin of that era and a reverse image emblematic of that president's life.") These coins can be bought as collectibles or as bullion investments. Special collector versions are offered in Proof format. (All shown at 1.5x actual size)

How Much Are My Gold Bullion Coins Worth?

Your gold bullion coins will typically be bought for a small discount to the net metal value of the coin. This is especially true of the older, less frequently traded issues. American Eagle gold coins will probably bring very close to or slightly higher than spot gold price. Seek multiple offers for your coins, as the prices bullion dealers are willing to pay can vary depending on their current needs.

Gold Bars

Gold bars come in many shapes and sizes, from 1/10 ounce to 1 kilogram (32.15 ounces). Some of the more popular makers include Credit Suisse, Engelhard, and Johnson Matthey. Selling your gold bars can be more difficult than selling coins, as their purity is less certain.

Some gold pieces are very popular as collectibles, and bring huge premiums over their gold value. Others are priced as precious metal and have no extra value to collectors. Still others, like this Johnson Matthey one-ounce ingot commemorating the Tolukuma gold mine in Papua, New Guinea, fall somewhere in between. (This ingot sold for about twice its bullion value in 2006.)

Smaller bars can usually be sold for close to the spot price without verification. Larger bars may require verification of purity to consummate a sale.

Gold bars and ingots vary in their weight and purity, and they hail from all over the world. For years they have been a common way to store, buy, and sell this precious metal.

NUMISMATICS—RARE GOLD AND SILVER COINS

The first gold coins were stuck by King Croesus of Lydia around 560 B.C. Ancient Greece and Rome produced gold coins for centuries, as well. For more than 2,500 years, gold coins were the primary global currency. Wealth was measured in gold and silver. In the United States, a $20 gold coin contained $20 worth of gold. Today, money is represented by numbers on a balance sheet. Simply press a few buttons and the money moves from one account to another. Gold and silver coins—relics of the old financial system—are highly valued by collectors.

Vintage U.S. gold coins were produced from 1795 to 1933. The first struck by the federal government were $5 and $10 gold pieces. These are highly desirable and are worth tens of thousands of dollars.

The United States struck silver coins for circulation from 1792 to 1969. In the 1700s and 1800s, the Mint made odd (to today's eye) silver denominations including the three-cent piece, the half dime, and the twenty-cent piece. More common were the dime, quarter, half dollar, and dollar coins. Dimes and quarters were debased from silver to copper-nickel in 1965.

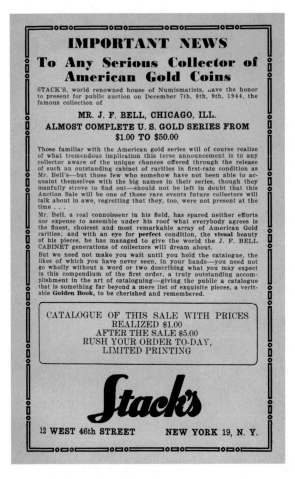

Rare gold coins have always captured the attention of collectors. This 1944 advertisement announced the sale of the J.F. Bell Collection by Stack's of New York.

Half dollars were reduced from the traditional 90% silver to 40% from 1965 to 1969, with a final coinage of 40% silver halves issued in Proof and Mint sets in 1970. Since then the regular-issue half dollar has been copper-nickel.

Over the years silver and gold coins have been struck for circulation (and as commemoratives) at seven different mints in the United States: Philadelphia, Denver, New Orleans, Carson City, San Francisco, Dahlonega, and Charlotte. They were struck in the following denominations:

Silver: $0.03 (silver three-cent piece, or *trime*); $0.05 (*half dime*); $0.10 (*dime*); $0.20 (*twenty-cent piece*); $0.25 (*quarter dollar*); $0.50 (*half dollar*); $1 (*silver dollar*)

Gold: $1 (*gold dollar*); $2.50 (called a *quarter eagle*); $3; $4 (very rare pattern coins, never struck for circulation); $5 (*half eagle*); $10 (*eagle*); $20 (*double eagle*); $50 (very rare pattern coins and some commemoratives, never struck for circulation)

In addition, the U.S. Mint operated a facility in Manila, in the Philippines, when that country was under American control. Today you can find coins with the dual legends UNITED STATES OF AMERICA and FIL-IPINAS, and exotic images of blacksmiths and volcanoes. Many of these coins, including silver 10-centavos, 20-centavos, 50-centavos, and pesos, were brought back to the States by American servicemen returning from World War II. Their collectible value is greater than their silver value.

The Philippines were acquired by the United States in 1899 as part of the treaty with Spain that ended the Spanish-American War. Over the next few decades (into the 1940s), the United States struck coins for use in the islands. The retail market for such coins is covered annually in the *Guide Book of United States Coins*. (coins shown at 1.5x actual size)

Many U.S. gold and silver coins are quite common and trade for a small numismatic premium over their melt value. Others are extremely rare and sell for millions of dollars. The auction record for a U.S. gold coin is more than $7 million, set in 2002 for a 1933 double eagle.

In July 2002 this 1933 double eagle (once owned by King Farouk of Egypt) was sold at auction for $7,590,020—the highest price ever paid for a single coin.

In 1933 the U.S. Mint struck nearly 450,000 double eagles like this one, but when President Franklin Roosevelt made gold bullion illegal to own, the coins, still at the Mint, were ordered to be melted. Today only 13 are known to have escaped the destruction. Collectively they are ranked No. 3 among the 100 Greatest U.S. Coins, in the book of the same name. (shown at 2x actual size)

Dozens of books have been written about rare gold and silver coins. The *Encyclopedia of U.S. Gold Coins 1795–1933*, by Jeff Garrett and Ron Guth, is one of the most complete studies on gold pieces. The book contains a photograph of every gold coin struck at the U.S. mints, along with rarity information, market notes, and other expert observations. The *Guide Book of Morgan Silver Dollars*, by Q. David Bowers, is a popular reference that has been updated in several editions since 2004.

An important book for pricing is the *Handbook of United States Coins* (popularly known as the "Blue Book"). This annual guide has wholesale values (how much coin dealers are paying, on average) for every U.S. coin in most collectible grades.

The value of rare coins is highly dependent on their condition. Pristine examples can sell for many times what a well-worn coin would bring. Choice examples often are graded (and certified as genuine) by an independent grading service before being sold into the retail market. These services are called "independent" because they grade coins neutrally, as a third party—representing neither the seller nor the buyer. Two of the largest grading companies are Professional Coin Grading Service (PCGS; online at collectors.com) and Numismatic Guaranty Corporation of America (NGC; online at ngccoin.com). Both have a network of dealers around the United States that can help you determine if your coins should be certified before sale. (Not every coin needs to be certified; a common coin in a common grade will often be sold "raw," or uncertified. However, unslabbed gold and silver coins should be carefully checked for authenticity, as many counterfeits plague the marketplace.) These dealers can also assist in shipping your coins to the grading services for evaluation.

"Slabbed" coins (professionally certified and graded by a third-party service).

BULLION WEIGHTS OF COMMON U.S. GOLD AND SILVER COINS

How much are your old gold and silver coins worth? If they're rare or in uncommonly attractive condition, they're probably worth more than their bullion value. If they're common and circulated, a dealer will likely buy them for a price near their actual gold or silver weight. These tables tell you how much value is in each of the larger gold coins struck by the U.S. Mint up to 1933, and the common silver denominations, depending on the spot price of gold or silver bullion. (Undamaged gold dollars, $2.50, $3, and $4 gold pieces, and older gold coins are always worth more than their gold value, because of collector demand. Likewise, all silver half dimes and three-cent and twenty-cent pieces also have higher numismatic value.) AGW stands for Actual Gold Weight, and ASW for Actual Silver Weight.

Gold Price Per Ounce	$5 (Half Eagle) Liberty Head 1839–1908 Indian Head 1908–1929 AGW .24187 oz.	$10 (Eagle) Liberty Head 1838–1907 Indian Head 1907–1933 AGW .48375 oz.	$20 (Double Eagle) 1849–1933 AGW .96750 oz.
$800	193.50	387.00	774.00
825	199.54	399.09	798.19
850	205.59	411.19	822.38
875	211.64	423.28	846.56
900	217.68	435.38	870.75
925	223.73	447.47	894.94
950	229.78	459.56	919.13
975	235.82	471.66	943.31
1,000	241.87	483.75	967.50
1,025	247.92	495.84	991.69
1,050	253.96	507.94	1,015.88
1,075	260.01	520.03	1,040.06
1,100	266.06	532.13	1,064.25
1,125	272.10	544.22	1,088.44
1,150	278.15	556.31	1,112.63
1,175	284.20	568.41	1,136.81
1,200	290.24	580.50	1,161.00
1,225	296.29	592.59	1,185.19

Gold Price Per Ounce	$5 (Half Eagle) Liberty Head 1839–1908 Indian Head 1908–1929 AGW .24187 oz.	$10 (Eagle) Liberty Head 1838–1907 Indian Head 1907–1933 AGW .48375 oz.	$20 (Double Eagle) 1849–1933 AGW .96750 oz.
1,250	302.34	604.69	1,209.38
1,275	308.38	616.78	1,233.56
1,300	314.43	628.88	1,257.75
1,325	320.48	640.97	1,281.94
1,350	326.52	653.06	1,306.13
1,375	332.57	665.16	1,330.31
1,400	338.62	677.25	1,354.50
1,425	344.66	689.34	1,378.69
1,450	350.71	701.44	1,402.88
1,475	356.76	713.53	1,427.06
1,500	362.81	725.63	1,451.25
1,525	368.85	737.72	1,475.44
1,550	374.90	749.81	1,499.63
1,575	380.95	761.91	1,523.81
1,600	386.99	774.00	1,548.00
1,625	393.04	786.09	1,572.19
1,650	399.09	798.19	1,596.38
1,675	405.13	810.28	1,620.56
1,700	411.18	822.38	1,644.75
1,725	417.23	834.47	1,668.94
1,750	423.27	846.56	1,693.13
1,775	429.32	858.66	1,717.31
1,800	435.37	870.75	1,741.50
1,825	441.41	882.84	1,765.69
1,850	447.46	894.94	1,789.88
1,875	453.51	907.03	1,814.06
1,900	459.55	919.13	1,838.25
1,925	465.60	931.22	1,862.44
1,950	471.65	943.31	1,886.63
1,975	477.69	955.41	1,910.81
2,000	483.74	967.50	1,935.00

Common-date half eagles ($5 gold coins), at actual size.

Common-date eagles ($10 gold coins), at actual size.

Common-date double eagles ($20 gold coins), at actual size.

Dimes, quarters, half dollars, and dollars minted prior to 1965 are .900 fine silver. These coins can be bought and sold in bulk—even in bags of $1,000 face value. Half dollars minted from 1965 to 1970 are .400 fine silver; these, too, can be bought and sold as commodities. So-called war nickels—the five-cent pieces minted from 1943 to 1945—also contained silver, as a substitute for the coin's nickel (which was being rationed as a critical war-effort material). These coins, even as small as they are, have enough silver in them to be valuable (with .05626 ounce of silver, each war nickel is worth $1.13 when spot is $20/ounce).

Silver Price Per Ounce	Wartime Nickel .05626 oz.	Dime .07234 oz.	Quarter Dollar .18084 oz	Half Dollar .36169 oz.	Silver Clad Half Dollar .14792 oz.	Silver Dollar .77344 oz.
$15	$0.84	$1.09	$2.71	$5.43	$2.22	$11.60
16	0.90	1.16	2.89	5.79	2.37	12.38
17	0.96	1.23	3.07	6.15	2.51	13.15
18	1.01	1.30	3.26	6.51	2.66	13.92
19	1.07	1.37	3.44	6.87	2.81	14.70
20	1.13	1.45	3.62	7.23	2.96	15.47
21	1.18	1.52	3.80	7.60	3.11	16.24
22	1.24	1.59	3.98	7.96	3.25	17.02
23	1.29	1.66	4.16	8.32	3.40	17.79
24	1.35	1.74	4.34	8.68	3.55	18.56
25	1.41	1.81	4.52	9.04	3.70	19.34
26	1.46	1.88	4.70	9.40	3.85	20.11
27	1.52	1.95	4.88	9.77	3.99	20.88
28	1.58	2.03	5.06	10.13	4.14	21.66
29	1.63	2.10	5.24	10.49	4.29	22.43
30	1.69	2.17	5.43	10.85	4.44	23.20
31	1.74	2.24	5.61	11.21	4.59	23.98
32	1.80	2.31	5.79	11.57	4.73	24.75
33	1.86	2.39	5.97	11.94	4.88	25.52
34	1.91	2.46	6.15	12.30	5.03	26.30
35	1.97	2.53	6.33	12.66	5.18	27.07
36	2.03	2.60	6.51	13.02	5.33	27.84
37	2.08	2.68	6.69	13.38	5.47	28.62
38	2.14	2.75	6.87	13.74	5.62	29.39
39	2.19	2.82	7.05	14.11	5.77	30.16
40	2.25	2.89	7.23	14.47	5.92	30.94
41	2.31	2.97	7.41	14.83	6.06	31.71
42	2.36	3.04	7.60	15.19	6.21	32.48
43	2.42	3.11	7.78	15.55	6.36	33.26

Silver Price Per Ounce	Wartime Nickel .05626 oz.	Dime .07234 oz.	Quarter Dollar .18084 oz	Half Dollar .36169 oz.	Silver Clad Half Dollar .14792 oz.	Silver Dollar .77344 oz.
44	2.48	3.18	7.96	15.91	6.51	34.03
45	2.53	3.26	8.14	16.28	6.66	34.80
46	2.59	3.33	8.32	16.64	6.80	35.58
47	2.64	3.40	8.50	17.00	6.95	36.35
48	2.70	3.47	8.68	17.36	7.10	37.13
49	2.76	3.54	8.86	17.72	7.25	37.90
50	2.81	3.62	9.04	18.08	7.40	38.67

Various common silver coins, shown at actual size.

Frequently Seen Older World Gold Coins

Gold coins have been struck in Europe and around the world for centuries. Pictured are some of the more common types you might own. Advice for selling them is similar to that for selling your U.S. gold coins.

German 10 marks and 20 marks (from various German states).

British sovereigns.

French 20 francs, 50 francs, and 100 francs.

Swiss 20 francs.

Mexican 10 pesos and 20 pesos.

How much are your old gold coins worth? If they're rare or in uncommonly attractive condition, they're likely worth much more than their bullion value. If they're common and circulated, a dealer will probably buy them for a price near their gold weight. This table tells you how much gold is in each of these common world gold coins.

Nation	Description	Denomination	Dates	(grams)	Fineness	(mm)	(troy oz.)
Australia	Nugget	$15	1986 to date	3.1103	1.000	16.10	0.1000
Australia	Nugget	$25	1986 to date	7.7508	1.000	20.10	0.2500
Australia	Nugget	$50	1986 to date	15.5017	1.000	25.10	0.5000
Australia	Nugget	$100	1986 to date	31.1035	1.000	32.10	1.0000
Austria	ducat	1 ducat	1901 to 1915	3.4909	0.986	20.00	0.1107
Austria	ducats	4 ducats	1901 to 1915	13.9636	0.986	40.00	0.4426
Austria	corona	10 corona	1905 to 1912	3.3875	0.900	19.00	0.0980
Austria	corona	20 corona	1901 to 1915	6.7751	0.900	21.00	0.1960
Austria	corona	100 corona	1908 to 1915	33.8753	0.900	37.00	0.9802
Austria	schillings	200 sch	1991 to date	3.1100	1.000	16.00	0.1000
Austria	schillings	500 sch	1989 to date	7.7760	1.000	22.00	0.2500
Austria	schillings	1,000 sch	1994 to date	15.5500	1.000	28.00	0.4999
Austria	schillings	2,000 sch	1989 to date	31.1035	1.000	36.50	0.9999
Belgium	francs	20 francs	1865 to 1882	6.4516	0.900	21.50	0.1867
Canada	Maple Leaf	$50	1979 to date	31.1033	0.999	30.00	1.0000
Canada	Maple Leaf	$25	1979 to date	15.5170	0.999	25.00	0.5000
Canada	Maple Leaf	$10	1979 to date	7.7758	0.999	20.00	0.2500
Canada	Maple Leaf	$5	1979 to date	3.1103	0.999	16.00	0.1000
China	Panda	5 yuan	1983 to 2000	1.5552	1.000	14.00	0.0499
China	Panda	10 yuan	1983 to 2000	3.1103	1.000	14.00	0.0999
China	Panda	25 yuan	1983 to 2000	7.7758	1.000	22.00	0.2497
China	Panda	50 yuan	1983 to 2000	15.5517	1.000	27.00	0.4995
China	Panda	100 yuan	1983 to 2000	31.1035	1.000	32.00	0.9999
Columbia	pesos	5 pesos	1913 to 1930	7.9881	0.917	22.00	0.2355
France	francs	20 francs (Rooster)	1901 to 1914	6.4516	0.900	21.00	0.1867
Germany	marks	20 marks (Prussia)	1901 to 1913	7.9650	0.900	22.50	0.2305
Great Britain	sovereign	1/2 soveign	1901 to date	3.9940	0.917	19.30	0.1177
Great Britain	sovereign	1 sovereign	1901 to date	7.9881	0.917	22.00	0.2355
Great Britain	Britannia	£100	1987 to date	34.0500	0.917	32.70	1.0038
Great Britain	Britannia	£50	1987 to date	17.0250	0.917	27.00	0.5019
Great Britain	Britannia	£25	1987 to date	8.5130	0.917	22.00	0.2508
Great Britain	Britannia	£10	1987 to date	3.4120	0.917	16.50	0.1006
Hungary	korona	100 korona	1907 to 1908	33.8753	0.900	36.00	0.9802
Italy	lire	20 lire	1861 to 1897	6.4516	0.900	21.00	0.1867

Nation	Description	Denomination	Dates	(grams)	Fineness	(mm)	(troy oz.)
Mexico	pesos	50 pesos	1921 to 1947	41.6666	0.900	37.00	1.2056
Mexico	pesos	20 pesos	1917 to 1959	16.6666	0.900	27.50	0.4822
Mexico	pesos	10 pesos	1905 to 1959	8.3333	0.900	22.50	0.2411
Mexico	pesos	5 pesos	1905 to 1955	4.1666	0.900	19.00	0.1206
Mexico	pesos	2-1/2 pesos	1918 to 1948	2.0833	0.900	15.50	0.0603
Mexico	pesos	2 pesos	1919 to 1948	1.6666	0.900	13.00	0.0482
N.E. Indies	ducat	1 ducat	1901 to date	3.4940	0.983	21.00	0.1104
Netherlands	gulden	10 gulden	1911 to 1933	6.7290	0.900	22.50	0.1947
Russia	roubles	5 roubles	1901 to 1911	4.3013	0.900	18.00	0.1245
Russia	roubles	10 roubles	1901 to 1911	8.6026	0.900	22.00	0.2489
South Africa	Krugerrand	1 Krugerrand	1967 to date	33.9300	0.917	32.70	1.0003
South Africa	Krugerrand	1/2 Krugerrand	1980 to date	16.9650	0.917	27.00	0.5001
South Africa	Krugerrand	1/4 Krugerrand	1980 to date	8.4820	0.917	22.00	0.2501
South Africa	Krugerrand	1/10 Krugerrand	1980 to date	3.3930	0.917	16.50	0.1000
Switzerland	francs	20 francs	1901 to 1949	6.4516	0.900	21.00	0.1867

FREQUENTLY SEEN OLDER WORLD SILVER COINS

Most developed nations minted silver coins for circulation into the early 1960s, as did the United States. Today these coins are actively sought by numismatists around the world. Many European coins were brought to the United States as souvenirs after the world wars, and these can sometimes be found among service members' personal effects. Collectors look for specific dates and mints to build complete collections (for example, of British shillings), or they might focus on a particular size of coin (e.g., dime-sized or dollar-sized), or they might try to collect one coin from every country. Common-date silver coins are also bought and sold in bulk, by actual silver weight, with no regard to their dates and conditions. A dealer will typically buy at some percentage below silver spot price, to later resell at some percentage above. Following are the actual silver weights of some commonly seen foreign silver coins. (For a much more comprehensive listing, see R.S. Yeoman's *Catalog of Modern World Coins, 1850–1964*, 14th edition, pages 499–509.) To calculate the silver value of these coins, simply multiply their "troy oz. silver" weight by the current spot price.

Country Name and Dates	Denom.	Fineness	Troy Oz. Silver
Australia			
1910–45	3 pence	0.9250	0.0419
	6 pence	0.9250	0.0838
	1 shilling	0.9250	0.1689
	1 florin	0.9250	0.3363
	1 crown	0.9250	0.8411
1946–64	3 pence	0.5000	0.0226
	6 pence	0.5000	0.0453
	1 shilling	0.5000	0.0908
	1 florin	0.5000	0.1818
Austria			
1780	Maria Theresa thaler	0.8333	0.7520
1857–68	1 vereinsthaler	0.9000	0.5358
	2 vereinsthaler	0.9000	1.0717
1858–67	5 kreuzer	0.3750	0.0161
	10 kreuzer	0.5000	0.0322
1868–72	10 kreuzer	0.4000	0.0214
	20 kreuzer	0.5000	0.0429
1857–92	1/4 florin	0.5208	0.0895
	1 florin	0.9000	0.3572
	2 florin	0.9000	0.7144
1892–1916	1 krone	0.8350	0.1342
	2 kronen	0.8350	0.2685
	5 kronen	0.9000	0.6944
1924	1 schilling	0.8000	0.1800
1925–38	1/2 schilling	0.6400	0.0617
	1 schilling	0.6400	0.1235
	2 schilling	0.6400	0.2469
	5 schilling	0.8350	0.4027
1960–68	5 schilling	0.6400	0.1070
1957–73	10 schilling	0.6400	0.1543
1955–73	25 schilling	0.8000	0.3344
1959–73	50 schilling	0.9000	0.5787

Country Name and Dates	Denom.	Fineness	Troy Oz. Silver
Belgium			
1865–1918	50 centimes	0.8350	0.0671
	1 franc	0.8350	0.1342
	2 francs	0.8350	0.2685
	5 francs	0.9000	0.7234
1933–35	20 francs	0.6800	0.2405
	50 francs	0.6800	0.4810
1939–40	50 francs	0.8350	0.5369
1948–60	20 francs	0.8350	0.2148
	50 francs	0.8350	0.3356
	100 francs	0.8350	0.4832
Canada			
1858–1910	5 cents	0.9250	0.0346
	10 cents	0.9250	0.0691
	20 cents	0.9250	0.1382
	25 cents	0.9250	0.1728
	50 cents	0.9250	0.3456
1910–19	5 cents	0.9250	0.0347
	10 cents	0.9250	0.0694
	25 cents	0.9250	0.1734
	50 cents	0.9250	0.3469
1920–67	5 cents	0.8000	0.0300
	10 cents	0.8000	0.0600
	25 cents	0.8000	0.1500
	50 cents	0.8000	0.3000
	1 dollar	0.8000	0.6000
Denmark			
1874–1958	10 ore	0.4000	0.0186
	25 ore	0.6000	0.0467
	50 ore	0.6000	0.0965
	1 krone	0.8000	0.1929
	2 kroner	0.8000	0.3858
1960, 64	5 kroner	0.8000	0.4372

Country Name and Dates	Denom.	Fineness	Troy Oz. Silver
France			
1848–66	20 centimes	0.9000	0.0289
	50 centimes	0.9000	0.0723
	1 franc	0.9000	0.1446
	2 francs	0.9000	0.2893
	5 francs	0.9000	0.7234
1866–1920	20 centimes	0.9000	0.0289
	50 centimes	0.8350	0.0671
	1 franc	0.8350	0.1342
	2 francs	0.9000	0.2893
	5 francs	0.9000	0.7234
1929–39	10 francs	0.6800	0.2186
	20 francs	0.6800	0.4372
1960–69	5 francs	0.8350	0.3221
Germany			
1873–1919	20 pfennig	0.9000	0.0322
	50 pfennig	0.9000	0.0804
	1 mark	0.9000	0.1608
1924–33	1 mark	0.5000	0.0804
	2 mark	0.5000	0.1608
	3 mark	0.5000	0.2411
	5 mark	0.5000	0.4019
1933–39	2 mark	0.6250	0.1608
	5 mark	0.9000	0.4019
Germany–Federal Republic			
1951–74	5 deutsche mark	0.6250	0.2250
Great Britain			
1837–1920	3 pence	0.9250	0.0420
	4 pence	0.9250	0.0561
	6 pence	0.9250	0.0841
	1 shilling	0.9250	0.1682
	1 florin	0.9250	0.3364
	1/2 crown	0.9250	0.4204

Country Name and Dates	Denom.	Fineness	Troy Oz. Silver
	2 florins	0.9250	0.6727
	1 crown	0.9250	0.8409
1895–1935	trade dollar	0.9000	0.7800
1920–46	3 pence	0.5000	0.0227
	6 pence	0.5000	0.0455
	1 shilling	0.5000	0.0909
	2 shillings / 1 florin	0.5000	0.1818
	1/2 crown	0.5000	0.2273
	1 crown	0.5000	0.4545
Italy			
1863–1917	20 centesimi	0.8350	0.0268
	50 centesimi	0.8350	0.0671
	1 lira	0.8350	0.1342
	2 lire	0.8350	0.2685
	5 lire	0.9000	0.7234
1926–41	5 lire	0.8350	0.1342
	10 lire	0.8350	0.2685
1927–34	20 lire	0.8000	0.3858
1928	20 lire (commem)	0.6000	0.3858
1936–41	20 lire	0.8000	0.5144
1958–2001	500 lire	0.8350	0.2953
Japan			
1870–71	5 sen	0.8000	0.0322
	10 sen	0.8000	0.0643
	20 sen	0.8000	0.1286
	50 sen	0.8000	0.3215
1873–1906	5 sen	0.8000	0.0347
	10 sen	0.8000	0.0693
	20 sen	0.8000	0.1387
	50 sen	0.8000	0.3467
1870–1914	1 yen	0.9000	0.7800
	trade dollar	0.9000	0.7875
1906–1917	10 sen	0.7200	0.0521

Country Name and Dates	Denom.	Fine-ness	Troy Oz. Silver	Country Name and Dates	Denom.	Fine-ness	Troy Oz. Silver
	20 sen	0.8000	0.1042	1955–60	10 pesos	0.9000	0.8357
	50 sen	0.8000	0.2604	1957–67	1 peso	0.1000	0.0514
1922–38	50 sen	0.7200	0.1146	**Netherlands**			
1957–64	100 yen	0.6000	0.0926	1848–1945	5 cents	0.6400	0.0141
1964	1,000 yen	0.9250	0.5948		10 cents	0.6400	0.0288
Mexico					25 cents	0.6400	0.0736
1822–69	1/4 real	0.9027	0.0246	1840–1919	1/2 gulden	0.9450	0.1519
	1/2 real	0.9027	0.0491		1 gulden	0.9450	0.3038
	1 real	0.9027	0.0982		2-1/2 gulden	0.9450	0.7595
1863–1905	5 centavos	0.9027	0.0393	1921–45	1/2 gulden	0.7200	0.1157
	10 centavos	0.9027	0.0786		1 gulden	0.7200	0.2315
	20 centavos	0.9027	0.1571		2-1/2 gulden	0.7200	0.5787
1822–1905	2 reales / 25 centavos	0.9027	0.1964	1954–67	1 gulden	0.7200	0.1504
	4 reales / 50 centavos	0.9027	0.3929		2-1/2 gulden	0.7200	0.3472
				New Zealand			
1822–1914	8 reales / 1 peso	0.9027	0.7857	1933–49	3 pence	0.5000	0.0227
					6 pence	0.5000	0.0455
1905–18	10 centavos	0.8000	0.0643		1 shilling	0.5000	0.0909
	20 centavos	0.8000	0.1286		1 florin	0.5000	0.1818
	50 centavos	0.8000	0.3215		1/2 crown	0.5000	0.2273
1918–19	10 centavos	0.8000	0.0466		1 crown	0.5000	0.4545
	20 centavos	0.8000	0.0932	**Philippines**			
	50 centavos	0.8000	0.2331	1864–80	10 centimos	0.9000	0.0751
	1 peso	0.8000	0.4662		20 centimos	0.9000	0.1502
1919–45	10 centavos	0.7200	0.0386		50 centimos	0.9000	0.3756
	20 centavos	0.7200	0.0772	1880–85	10 centimos	0.8350	0.0679
	50 centavos	0.7200	0.1929		20 centimos	0.8350	0.1394
	1 peso	0.7200	0.3858		50 centimos	0.8350	0.3485
	2 pesos	0.9000	0.7716	1897	1 peso	0.9000	0.7234
1935	50 centavos	0.4200	0.1077	1903–06	10 centavos	0.9000	0.0779
1947–49	1 peso	0.5000	0.2251		20 centavos	0.9000	0.1558
	5 pesos	0.9000	0.8681		50 centavos	0.9000	0.3900
1950–54	5 pesos	0.7200	0.6431		1 peso	0.9000	0.7800
1955–59	5 pesos	0.7200	0.4170	1907–47	10 centavos	0.7500	0.0482

Country Name and Dates	Denom.	Fineness	Troy Oz. Silver
	20 centavos	0.7500	0.0965
	50 centavos	0.7500	0.2411
	1 peso	0.8000	0.5144
1961	1/2 peso	0.9000	0.3617
1961–64	1 peso	0.9000	0.7523
Poland			
1924–25	1 zloty	0.7500	0.1206
	2 zlote	0.7500	0.2411
	5 zloytch	0.9000	0.7234
1928–32	5 zloytch	0.7500	0.4340
1932–39	2 zlote	0.7500	0.2652
	5 zloytch	0.7500	0.2122
	10 zloytch	0.7500	0.5305
Russia			
1855–58	5 kopeks	0.8680	0.0289
	10 kopeks	0.8680	0.0577
	20 kopeks	0.8680	0.1157
	25 kopeks	0.8680	0.1446
	1/2 ruble	0.8680	0.2892
	1 ruble	0.8680	0.5785
1859–66	5 kopeks	0.7500	0.0250
	10 kopeks	0.7500	0.0500
	15 kopeks	0.7500	0.1000

Country Name and Dates	Denom.	Fineness	Troy Oz. Silver
	20 kopeks	0.7500	0.0145
1859–85	25 kopeks	0.8680	0.1446
	50 kopeks	0.8680	0.2893
	1 ruble	0.8680	0.5785
1867–1931	5 kopeks	0.5000	0.0145
	10 kopeks	0.5000	0.0289
	15 kopeks	0.5000	0.0434
	20 kopeks	0.5000	0.0579
1886–1931	25 kopeks	0.9000	0.1446
	50 kopeks	0.9000	0.2893
	1 ruble	0.9000	0.5786
Switzerland			
1850–57	1/2 franc	0.9000	0.0723
	1 franc	0.9000	0.1447
	2 francs	0.9000	0.2894
1850–1928	5 francs	0.9000	0.7234
1860–61	1/2 franc	0.8000	0.1286
	1 franc	0.8000	0.2572
1874–1967	1/2 franc	0.8350	0.0671
	1 franc	0.8350	0.1342
	2 francs	0.8350	0.2685
1931–69	5 francs	0.8350	0.4027

WHERE DO I SELL MY GOLD AND SILVER?

With the barrage of advertising from companies offering to buy your precious metal it can be difficult deciding where to sell. Here are some options to consider.

THE INTERNET

There are literally thousands of buyers on the Internet trying to purchase your gold and silver. One of the most prominent companies offering to buy unwanted scrap gold ran an ad during the 2009 Super Bowl. Comparison shopping has found most of the firms offer less than 50% of the true melt

Great Britain shilling.

France 5 francs.

Australia florin.

Japan 100 Yen.

Germany 5 marks.

Switzerland franc.

Belgium 2 francs.

Netherlands gulden.

Mexico peso.

Canada 50 cents.

value of gold, and some as little as 15% or less. Another downside: you must take the risk of sending your property through the mail to someone you do not know.

Search for "gold buyer," "selling silver coins," and similar phrases on the Internet.

Gold and silver *bullion* (as opposed to scrap) can be sold to buyers found on the Internet with better results. Because it is easier to determine the value of gold and silver bars and coins, bullion houses will work on closer margins in most cases. Check with several companies to get quotes. The only problem with selling bullion to a company found on the Internet is the safety issue. You will be required to ship your material to a complete stranger. Be sure to get multiple references and opt for a reputable firm rather than just trying to get the highest price.

There are thousands of rare-coin dealers in the United States. Most have at least a nominal Internet presence. (See below for more about coin shops.) One of the most common uses of the Internet when selling rare coins is to locate a dealer in your area. You can also search the web by specialty. The Internet is a valuable tool, but you should always be wary of fraud.

Two organizations that can connect you with reputable coin dealers online: the American Numismatic Association (money.org) and the Professional Numismatists Guild (pngdealers.com).

HOTEL BUYERS

You've probably seen them—splashy, full-page or multiple-page ads offering to pay the absolute highest dollar for your gold, silver, rare coins, collectibles, and anything else of value. Often the company will set up in a hotel ballroom or other large public space. Remember, these ads and venues are expensive, and their cost is usually passed on to *you*, the person selling. In many instances you will receive less than 50% of the true melt value for your gold and silver. By doing your homework and knowing the value of your holdings, you might fare better with some companies. Be careful when doing business with any company that is only in town for a few days. If a problem evolves, your chances of recovery are minimal.

PAWN SHOPS

Nearly every city and town has pawn shops that serve the unbanked community with short-term loans. Most also purchase gold, silver, and diamonds. As you would expect, pawn shops are usually high-profit-margin operations. Expect to receive 50% to 75% of the melt value for

scrap precious metals. Unless a pawn shop has an expert on staff to handle gold and silver bullion or rare coins, it probably won't be a good venue to sell either of those items.

COIN SHOPS

There are thousands of coin shops in the United States. Many also deal in precious metals, and have for decades. In general, coin shops work on a much closer profit margin than the buyers cited above. A recent phone survey found that most coin shops pay 75% to 80% of the melt value for scrap or unwanted gold from the public. Larger quantities will bring a higher percentage.

Most coin shops in the United States also have very active gold and silver bullion operations. Prices you will receive can vary greatly from company to company. When selling, it is always good to get quotes from several dealers. If you live in a small community your town may have only one coin shop, or none at all. It might be very worthwhile to travel to the nearest large town to sell your gold and silver. Again, call for quotes to make that determination.

Selling rare coins in a coin shop is very easy, but you should do your homework first. Check for professional references, and make sure the dealer has expertise in the field. If you visit a coin shop and there are no gold or silver coins in the showcases, you are probably in the wrong place. Ask the dealer about third-party grading and certification if you believe you have high-quality or unusually rare coins. Most dealers will be happy to have the coins certified, and then tender an offer based on the results.

You also have the comfort of knowing the company occupies a permanent physical location and will be around in case of disputes or problems. Many coin dealers are members of national organizations that offer mediation if a disagreement arises. Look for dealers who have membership in the Professional Numismatists Guild (the PNG, online at pngdealers. com) and/or the American Numismatic Association (the ANA, online at money.org).

AUCTIONS

Auction venues are another option when considering how to sell rare coins. Some sellers list items on popular online sites such as eBay. These auction sites can be difficult for beginning sellers, however, as you need at least some knowledge of digital photography, computers, shipping, insurance, and other business factors. Also, fraud can be a problem, with some buyers attempting to use stolen credit cards or indulging in other deceptive practices. For important, rare gold and silver coins there are numerous large auction firms in the United States that will offer their services to sell your coins. Typical commission rates run about 20% to 25% of the net selling price at auction. Many sales are held around the country in conjunction with major rare-coin shows.

Hobby newspapers have information on coin shows nationwide—including in your city or state.

Visiting a coin show will put you in touch with dozens or even hundreds of coin dealers all gathered in a single place. Many will be eager to buy your gold and silver.

COIN SHOWS

Every weekend in the United States at least one rare-coin convention takes place. Some are only one-day events. Others, like the Whitman Coin and Collectibles Expos (WhitmanExpo.com) held in Baltimore and Philadelphia, run nearly a week. Large shows can have more than 500 dealers from around the world in attendance. These can be an excellent opportunity to find out what your rare gold and silver coins are worth. You can ask multiple dealers about the value of your holdings. Make sure to get more than one offer before selling. You may also see similar coins for sale at the convention, which will give you an idea of value. For a listing of shows around the country, purchase a copy of *Coin World* (CoinWorldOnline.com) or *Numismatic News* (NumismaticNews.net). Both have extensive coverage of shows held annually.

REFINERIES

Refineries will pay the most for precious metals, but they usually only deal in very large amounts. Most also require a longstanding business relationship or a referral. Typically refiners pay around 98.5% of actual melt value. These venues are where most of the gold and silver purchased by the buyers described above ends up. The metal is refined into bars and sold to the investment or jewelry industry.

SHIPPING COINS OR BULLION BY MAIL

Most buyers of your coins or bullion will give you step-by-step instructions on how to ship your merchandise to them. Safety should be your primary concern. U.S. Postal Service Registered Mail is probably the most often used service for sending high-value packages. Insurance for the package can be purchased for nominal cost. Registered Mail is seldom lost. One problem with Registered Mail is that packages must be very carefully wrapped and some assistance may be required to properly conform to Post Office rules. FedEx is another option for shipping, but is somewhat less secure. Regardless of your shipping option, be sure to double-box and tightly package the contents.

Knowledge is power when purchasing precious metals!

BUYING PRECIOUS METALS

P urchasing gold, silver, and platinum as a way of protecting wealth has become very popular in recent months. Headline after headline talks about the incredible rise of the annual deficit and the national debt. The United States faces yearly trillion-dollar-plus shortfalls for the foreseeable future. Many people worry this will lead to higher interest rates and rampant inflation. Many countries over the last several decades have experienced hyperinflation. One of the best ways to hedge against such a calamity is to own precious metals. Gold, for example, has held its value as a financial tool for centuries. Empires have come and gone, along with their currencies. Gold, however, is universally recognized as a store of permanent value.

The German Empire was the greatest European power in the early 1900s, and its gold coins (shown here 2x actual size) were known and respected far and wide. In the fires of World War I, mighty Germany was toppled, and its emperor, Wilhelm II, was dethroned. Kingdoms and empires rise and fall. Gold and silver are more permanent.

"WHAT KIND OF PRECIOUS METAL SHOULD I BUY?"

Although many people are becoming interested in buying precious metals as a hedge in their investment portfolio, few know how to do it. Gold, silver, and platinum come in many shapes and sizes. There are bars, coins, jewelry, gold and silver funds, and more. Some people prefer to buy shares of mining companies, while most prefer to own the actual, physical metal. For individual investors, *coins* make the most sense. They can be purchased and sold in any quantity—this can be handy in the case of short-term cash needs. The purity and weight of coins are guaranteed by their issuing country. Coins are easy to store and ship, as well.

BULLION COINS

In the United States the most popular bullion coins are the American Eagles. They are struck in a one-ounce format for silver; and in four different sizes each for gold and platinum (1/10 ounce, 1/4 ounce, 1/2 ounce, and 1 ounce). The American Eagle bullion issues are made of .9993 fine silver; .9167 fine gold; and .9995 fine platinum. (The U.S. Mint also makes .9999 fine American Buffalo bullion coins, and .9999 fine First Spouse bullion coins. These are discussed in chapter 5.)

Precious metals come in many forms. As an investment, bullion coins are best.

Many other countries also issue bullion coins. Among them are Canada, Australia, Great Britain, China, Austria, Mexico, and several others. Those of some other countries are struck in pure gold (.999 fine, or finer), including the Canadian Maple Leaf issues.

HOW TO BUY BULLION COINS

Whether you have a few hundred dollars to invest, or millions, bullion coins can be purchased relatively easily. Most local coin shops deal in bullion and can offer a variety of choices. The safest option when trying to find a dealer is to look for membership in the American Numismatic Association (ANA, online at money.org) and/or the Professional Numismatist Guild (PNG, pngdealers.com). Members of these groups must adhere to strict codes of ethics. In the case of a dispute, these organizations will mediate your claim.

For large transactions, the seller may require a deposit at purchase and the balance due upon delivery of the coins. Be sure to check references on any dealer when buying coins for future delivery. This can be a problem for both buyers and sellers with the value of gold, for example, being over $1,200 per ounce. Even a small transaction means large dollar amounts trading hands, in most cases. Part of the reason to purchase precious metal is the security of owning the actual metal, and not a piece of paper.

TIP: ALWAYS TAKE POSSESSION!

Never buy platinum, gold, or silver and leave it in storage with the company you purchased it from. There have been cases of fraud by companies that claimed to be holding precious metals for safe keeping. You can easily avoid such fraud by taking possession and storing your bullion in a bank safety-deposit box. Remember, metals are a hedge against financial calamity, and having physical possession is very important.

There are also dozens of bullion dealers around the country who can sell you coins. Many advertise on TV and radio. Most are legitimate, but always check references when making a large transaction. One problem with many of the advertising companies is their telemarketing operations. After making a purchase of precious metals, you will probably be pitched on buying something else—usually higher-profit-margin products such as rare coins, third-party certified coins, and world-mint products. Many of these collectibles are interesting, but if your main concern is hedging against problems with the American economy, you should stick with bullion coins. Rare coins are great, but there is much to learn before you make a purchase.

"How Much Should I Pay for Bullion?"

The price of precious metals can vary greatly based on supply and demand. In the last year or so, gold coins sold faster than the U.S. Mint could make them. Premiums usually vary from 6 to 10% above spot for the American Eagle issues. The smaller fractional issues (the 1/10-, 1/4-, and 1/2-ounce pieces) trade for a higher percentage over melt. Expect to pay considerably more *per ounce* for a 1/10-ounce gold coin than for a 1-ounce gold coin.

Make sure there are no hidden costs or commissions. If the transaction gets complicated, call another seller—the market is competitive enough for you to find a good deal.

As with any large purchase, you should get several quotes before buying. Also, make sure the dealer you have contacted also *buys* bullion coins. You will need a place to sell at some point in the future.

Tip: Get a Buy/Sell Quote

When asking for prices, get a buy/sell quote for the item you are interested in. This may help you get a lower price. Platinum, gold, and silver values fluctuate daily, so check the current price before making a purchase. Bullion prices can be found in most newspapers and are easily found on the Internet. Search for "gold spot value," "silver bullion price," or similar terms.

10 Important Things to Know When Buying Bullion

1. Some states still charge sales or use taxes for bullion purchases. Many do not. Check with your accounting professional for advice on how to handle the tax issue.
2. There are reporting requirements to the IRS when selling large amounts (more than 20 ounces) of precious metals. Again, check with a tax professional for advice on current tax laws that may affect your transactions.
3. The safest place to store bullion is your safety deposit box. Large amounts of platinum, gold, and silver can fit in a small box, and the annual charge is minimal.
4. Insurance for the contents of safety deposit boxes is quite inexpensive. Check with your insurance provider for quotes.
5. Protect yourself from identity theft. Never give credit-card information, Social Security numbers, or bank-account information to anyone that is not known to you, over the phone. Be especially wary of overseas transactions.
6. Never buy bullion coins on margin or credit. This can be quite risky, and you do not have physical possession of the metal. Leave this option to the professionals.
7. Gold bars may be purchased, but when you go to resell them your buyer might require an assay to determine their gold content. This can take time, and is costly. Smaller bars of 1 to 5 ounces are quite liquid if manufactured by a recognized refiner such as Engelhard or Credit Suisse.
8. Consider cost averaging if you are contemplating a large purchase of bullion. It is easy to get excited by the news headlines these days, and make a purchase on impulse. Study the market and make your purchases over a few months' time. This will help you avoid buying at peak prices. Many stock professionals use cost averaging for the same reason.
9. Avoid fraud. If you are offered something too good to be true, you can be sure that it is. Contact your state's attorney's office if you suspect fraud. Better safe than sorry.
10. If you store your precious metal at home, take security precautions including an alarm system, secure doors and windows, strong locks, and a fireproof safe. (But see no. 3, above.)

BUYING RARE COINS

Old coins are an interesting and tangible link to our past. Because they were objects of value, they were seldom discarded. From ancient Greece and Rome through the Middle Ages, the Renaissance, and the Industrial Revolution, coins have survived to provide a tapestry of human history. As a result, millions of people over the years have found that numismatics—the study of coins—is a richly rewarding and educational experience. Collecting coins can be both a satisfying hobby and a profitable investment.

Gold coins have been minted for centuries, dating back to the ancient Greeks.

There are dozens of ways to collect gold and silver coins. (For the purpose of this discussion, we won't explore platinum coins because of their limited use throughout history; see chapter 3.) Here are some of the more popular methods.

ANCIENT COINS

Coins were invented by the ancient Greeks in Ionia or Lydia, in what is modern-day Turkey, just after 700 BC. The invention of coinage meant the beginning of the end of barter and the start of international commerce. Greek and Roman coins are miniature sculptures of great beauty and historical interest. Many collectors are fascinated to purchase actual coins struck during the reigns of Alexander the Great, Julius Caesar, Augustus, Nero, and Marcus Aurelius. Most ancient gold coins start in price around $1,000. Important rarities can bring millions. There are dozens of dealers in the United States who specialize in ancient coinage. The American Numismatic Association and the Professional Numismatists Guild both maintain lists of member dealers and their areas of expertise, as does the International Association of Professional Numismatists (iapn-coins.org).

This is a 100-litra (or double decadrachm) gold coin of the ancient Greek city-state of Syracuse. It features the water nymph Arethusa and the demigod Heracles. In his book *100 Greatest Ancient Coins,* Harlan J. Berk calls this coin "a little gem, an example of great art in a small space." Berk ranks it as no. 19 among the 100 greatest of all ancient coins. "The face of Arethusa is exceptionally sweet," he writes. "She is shown here as a young goddess. Her hair is elaborately arranged and carefully engraved, as are the hairnet and jewelry, all without robbing the face of its fresh innocence." He describes the reverse as equally impressive. "The artist has here arranged the combat between Heracles and the lion to conform to the circular flan of the coin, giving the coin and the design a feeling of organic wholeness. The musculature of both Heracles and the lion is beautifully defined and creates a feeling of balance and dynamic symmetry." (actual size ~ 15 mm)

The masterpieces of Athens are perhaps the most famous of ancient coinage. The Greek city-state was itself famous throughout the civilized world, and its coins circulated widely. The Athenian silver decadrachm was known as an owl, from its reverse design (the animal symbolic of the goddess Athena). (actual size ~ 23 mm)

WORLD COINS

Gold and silver coins have been struck around the world for centuries. People who appreciate history, geography, language, and cultures will find unlimited opportunities in the field of world coins. Much of the economic history of the world is chronicled within numismatics. Most collectors focus on one country or time period—but let your imagination guide you in this exciting area of collecting.

This beautiful 20-mark gold coin was struck in Berlin for German New Guinea. "The bird of paradise was emblematic of the new colony," notes Richard Doty in *Money of the World: Coins That Made History*. (actual size 22 mm)

The following are some of the more commonly seen world gold coins. These can be bought as collectibles, or as bullion investments. Typically their prices are close to their gold value.

Austria 1 dukat (1857–1915). 0.1107 oz. actual gold.

Austria 20 corona (1892–1924). 0.1960 oz. actual gold.

Austria 10 corona (1892–1924). 0.0980 oz. actual gold.

Austria 4 dukaten (1857–1915). 0.4427 oz. actual gold.

Austria 100 corona (1892–1924). 0.9802 oz. actual gold.

Belgium 20 francs (1867–1914). 0.1867 oz. actual gold.

Canada $5 Maple Leaf. 0.1000 oz. actual gold.

Canada $20 Maple Leaf. 0.5000 oz. actual gold.

Canada $10 Maple Leaf. 0.2500 oz. actual gold.

China 1/10-ounce Panda. 0.1000 oz. actual gold.

Canada $50 Maple Leaf. 1.0000 oz. actual gold.

China 1/4-ounce Panda. 0.2500 oz. actual gold.

China 1/2-ounce Panda. 0.5000 oz. actual gold.

China 1-ounce Panda. 1.0000 oz. actual gold.

Great Britain sovereign (1838–1968, plus modern bullion issues). 0.2354 oz. actual gold.

Colombia 5 pesos (1862–1878 / 1885–1886 / 1913–1930). 0.1867 oz. / 0.1728 oz. / 0.2354 oz. actual gold.

Hungary 100 korona (1868–1916). 0.9802 oz. actual gold.

France 20 francs (1848–1914). 0.1867 oz. actual gold.

Italy 20 lire (1861–1927). 0.1867 oz. actual gold.

Germany 10 marks (1871–1915). 0.1152 oz. actual gold.

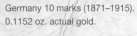

Mexico 2 pesos (1919–1947). 0.0482 oz. actual gold.

Mexico 2-1/2 pesos (1870–1905). 0.1190 oz. actual gold.

Mexico 5 pesos (1870–1905). 0.2380 oz. actual gold.

Mexico 10 pesos (1905–1959). 0.2411 oz. actual gold.

Mexico 20 pesos (1905–1959). 0.4823 oz. actual gold.

Mexico 50 pesos (1905–1959). 1.2056 oz. actual gold.

Netherlands 10 gulden (1875–1933). 0.1944 oz. actual gold.

Russia 5 rubles (1886–1897 / 1897–1911). 0.1867 oz. / 0.1245 oz. actual gold.

Russia 10 rubles (1886–1897 / 1897–1911). 0.3734 oz. / 0.2489 oz. actual gold.

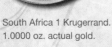

South Africa 1/10 Krugerrand. 0.1000 oz. actual gold.

South Africa 1/4 Krugerrand. 0.250 oz. actual gold.

South Africa 1/2 Krugerrand. 0.5000 oz. actual gold.

South Africa 1 Krugerrand. 1.0000 oz. actual gold.

Switzerland 20 francs (1883–1949). 0.1867 oz. actual gold.

UNITED STATES GOLD AND SILVER COINS

The first U.S. gold coins appeared in 1795, when $5 and $10 pieces were struck at the mint in Philadelphia. The coins feature a Capped Bust design on the obverse, and an eagle perched on an olive branch. The series is commonly referred to as "Small Eagle" gold coins. These usually sell for $20,000 to $100,000, depending on quality. Because of their historic importance as witnesses to the founding of our nation, they are highly desirable.

The following year, in 1796, $2.50 gold coins were minted. Only 963 examples of the first "No Stars" type were struck. Today there are only about 100 known in all grades, and they routinely sell for more than $100,000 each.

After the start of the California Gold Rush of 1848, the U.S. Mint began striking $1 and $20 gold coins, in 1849. The 1849 double eagle is unique, and it resides in the National Numismatic Collection of the Smithsonian Institution.

A new denomination, $3 gold coins, was minted from 1854 to 1889. This interesting series is highly collected and contains many exciting rarities, including the unique 1870-S $3 gold piece.

The largest gold coins ever produced by the U.S. Mint were $50 "slugs" first struck as pattern or experimental issues in 1877, and, later, among the Panama-Pacific commemorative issues of 1915. The 1877 patterns are represented by just two examples (each of a slightly different design) that also reside in the Smithsonian collection. Around 1,000 of the Panama-Pacific Exposition commemoratives were distributed in 1915. Today these large gold coins (weighing 2.5 ounces each) sell for $75,000 to $200,000 apiece.

Another exciting area of U.S. gold coinage are the many private-issue pieces struck from around 1830 to the 1860s. No state or territory had the authority to mint its own coins, but because of necessity, pieces of various shapes and sizes were struck in areas of the United States by assayers, bankers, and other private issuers. Most are quite rare, and sell for thousands of dollars.

This 1795 half eagle ($5 gold piece) was among the first gold coins struck by the U.S. Mint. Fewer than 10,000 were made. (shown 1.5x actual size)

Production of quarter eagles ($2.50 gold pieces) followed that of half eagles, in 1796. The first design had no stars on the obverse; they were added later in the year. (shown 1.5x actual size)

Gold dollars were first minted in 1849, shortly after the California Gold Rush started. (shown 1.5x actual size)

The unique 1849 double eagle is part of the Smithsonian's National Numismatic Collection. While the coin is not for sale, its value is estimated at $20 million in the third edition of *100 Greatest U.S. Coins*. (shown 1.5x actual size)

The $3 gold coin was struck from 1854 to 1889. According to the *Guide Book of United States Coins*, "The head on the obverse represents an Indian princess," while the reverse features American agriculture in a "wreath of tobacco, wheat, corn, and cotton." (shown 1.5x actual size)

"The year 1877 is remarkable for the beauty and diversity of its patterns," writes Q. David Bowers in *United States Pattern Coins*. He calls the $50 gold patterns of that year "large and impressive"—they measure two inches in diameter. (shown actual size)

Collecting rare U.S. gold coins is an exciting and rewarding area of numismatics. Because of their intrinsic value (metal content), gold coins are among the most sought after by collectors. There are more than 1,500 individual issues, however, and there is much to know before you make a purchase. One of the best pieces of numismatic advice ever given is "Buy the book before the coin." Dozens of references have been published over the years on the subject of U.S. gold coins. Here are some recommendations:

Akers, David W. *Gold Dollars (and Other Gold Denominations)*, Englewood, OH, 1975–1982.

Bowers, Q. David. *A California Gold Rush History, Featuring Treasure from the S.S. Central America*, Wolfeboro, NH, 2001.

Bowers, Q. David. *A Guide Book of Double Eagle Gold Coins*, Atlanta, GA, 2004.

Bowers, Q. David. *A Guide Book of Gold Dollars*, Atlanta, GA, 2011.

Bowers, Q. David. *United States Gold Coins: An Illustrated History*, Wolfeboro, NH, 1982.

Breen, Walter, and Gillio, Ronald. *California Pioneer Fractional Gold*, Santa Barbara, CA, 1983.

Breen, Walter. *Major Varieties of U.S. Gold Dollars (and Other Gold Denominations)*, Chicago, IL, 1964.

Dannreuther, John W., and Bass, Harry W. *Early U.S. Gold Coin Varieties*, Atlanta, GA, 2006.

Fivaz, Bill. *United States Gold Counterfeit Detection Guide*, Atlanta, GA, 2005.

Garrett, Jeff, and Guth, Ron. *Encyclopedia of U.S. Gold Coins, 1795–1933*, Atlanta, GA, 2008.

Kagin, Donald H. *Private Gold Coins and Patterns of the United States*, New York, NY, 1981.

Moran, Michael F. *Striking Change: The Great Artistic Collaboration of Theodore Roosevelt and Augustus Saint-Gaudens*, Atlanta, GA, 2008.

Coins struck in silver, alloyed with copper, were first made at the Philadelphia Mint in the 1790s. The first silver U.S. coins were the half dismes of 1792, followed by the 1794-dated half dime, half dollar, and dollar. Dimes, quarters, and half dollars made their appearance in 1796. As time went on, designs changed and evolved, as did weights and alloy standards. The silver three-cent piece, or trime, a new denomination, appeared in 1851. In 1873 the silver trade dollar was born, but lasted only until 1878 (plus later Proofs struck for collectors), followed by the even shorter-lived twenty-cent piece of 1875 and 1876 (plus two more years of Proofs for numismatists).

Generally, designs for early silver coins were similar across all denominations, with most issues of 1794 and 1795 having Flowing Hair (it is usual to capitalize motifs in numismatic text), later denominations having the Draped Bust style, and then the Capped Bust motif, followed by the long-lived Liberty Seated design, then in 1892 the Barber dime, quarter, and half dollar. In the meantime, the twenty-cent piece (1875), the trade dollar (1873), and the new silver dollar (the Morgan dollar of 1878) had their own motifs.

In 1916 artists in the private sector were commissioned to create the "Mercury" dime, Standing Liberty quarter, and Liberty Walking half dollar. All three went on to become extremely popular with collectors. In 1921 the Peace silver dollar, also designed by an outside sculptor, joined this illustrious group.

By 1964, silver was becoming expensive on international markets, and after that time the standard alloy of 90% silver and 10% copper was abandoned, although some silver-content half dollars were produced through 1970. Since then, occasional special coins and commemoratives in silver have been made for sale to collectors. Today, for coins used in general circulation, clad alloy replaces silver in such denominations as the dime, quarter, half dollar, and dollar, with the "golden dollar" of 2000 and beyond having a distinctive appearance.

"The Peace dollar design was the last step in the evolution of United States coinage from static 19th-century formalism to a more dynamic and diverse representation of America," writes Roger W. Burdette in the *Guide Book of Peace Dollars*. The coin was designed to honor the end of World War I. (shown actual size)

IMPORTANT THINGS TO KNOW WHEN BUYING RARE COINS

HOW VALUE IS DETERMINED

Surprisingly, *age* has very little to do with the value of a rare coin. The coin's rarity, condition, and historical significance play much larger roles when determining value. The last of the "classic" gold struck by the U.S. Mint, the 1933 $20 piece, holds the auction-record price for any coin ever sold, at more than $7,000,000.

The rarity of a coin is determined by the number of examples known to exist. There are many cases of particular coins being struck in large quantities, but because of melting over the years, very few are known today. Popularity of a series also plays an important part when determining value. Coins in a popular series will sell for more than coins in a series that few people collect.

Older coins are not necessarily more valuable. In Very Fine condition, a gold eagle from 1840 and one from 1932 are worth about the same.

CONDITION IS VITAL

After coins are struck by the Mint, they enter circulation. Portions of the design begin to wear away and the coins become less desirable to collectors. Some examples have been more carefully preserved since their striking, and never entered circulation. Although these coins are in mint condition (called Mint State, or Uncirculated), others factors come into play—such as the strength of the coin's strike, and whether it has "bag marks" (tiny nicks caused by contact with other coins in a mint bag).

THE IMPORTANCE OF CONDITION: A CASE STUDY

The 1904 $20 gold coin is a very common issue. In the lower states of preservation, its metal content is the most important element of its value. An About Uncirculated (AU-55) coin will sell for around $1,500 when gold is at $1,100 an ounce. A superb gem (Mint State–65 coin) would sell for more than $5,000. Because of the critical nature of condition when determining value, there are several independent companies that authenticate, grade, and certify rare coins. Among the largest are ANACS, Numismatic Guaranty Corporation of America (NGC), and the Professional Coin Grading Service (PCGS). These services have certified billions of dollars in coins over the last 25 years.

There are several excellent guide books that teach you about grading coins, including *The Official American Numismatic Association Grading Standards for United States Coins.*

The following is adapted from *Grading Coins by Photographs: An Action Guide for the Collector and Investor:*

Case Study: Grading 1839–1908 Liberty Head Half Eagles

MS-60 to 70 (Mint State)

Illustrated coin: 1847-C. MS-60. Here is an above-average strike with rich luster—exceptional quality for a Charlotte Mint coin at this grade. A tiny mark below the 4 (1847) may prompt otherwise conservative grading. Overall, this is a "find" for the specialist.

Obverse. At MS-60, some abrasion and contact marks are evident, most noticeably on the hair to the right of Miss Liberty's forehead and on the jaw. Luster is present, but may be dull or lifeless, and interrupted in patches. At MS-63, contact marks are few, and abrasion is very light. An MS-65 coin has only slight abrasion, and contact marks are so minute as to require magnification. Luster should be full and rich. Grades above MS-65 are defined by having fewer marks as perfection is approached.

Reverse. Comments apply as for the obverse, except that abrasion and contact marks are most noticeable on the eagle's neck and to the lower left of the shield.

VF-20, 30 (Very Fine)

Illustrated coin: 1858-C. VF-20.

Obverse. The higher-relief areas of hair are worn flat at VF-20, less so at VF-30. The hair to the right of the coronet is merged into heavy strands. The stars are flat at their centers.

Reverse. Feather detail is mostly worn away on the neck and legs, less so on the wings. The vertical shield stripes, being deeply recessed, remain bold.

BUYING COMMON-DATE U.S. GOLD AND SILVER COINS

In 1933 President Franklin D. Roosevelt signed Executive Order 6102, forbidding the "hoarding" of gold coins and bullion. This was done to protect the fragile banking system of the United States, which had been decimated by the Great Depression.

Although the law allowed anyone to keep up to $100 face value of gold coins, and any coins with recognized collector value, millions were turned in and melted. The gold bars at Fort Knox are the result of this great melt. Thousands of coins, however, found their way overseas to foreign banks. To this day, there is a continuous flow of these coins back to the United States. Most of the coins being repatriated are $10 and $20 gold pieces. There is an active market for these issues, and they trade more as a commodity than as rare coins.

Note that there is also demand from investors who believe that if financial conditions in the United States were to deteriorate badly, the U.S. government could once again consider "confiscation," and that these coins would be exempt. Do not let such rumors alarm you into making unwise purchase decisions.

TIP: DO NOT PANIC

Be aware that some firms strongly push the idea that the federal government might order the surrender of gold, and they suggest higher-profit-margin products to protect your assets. The chances of gold confiscation are remote, so do your research carefully before buying coins based on this fear.

Common-date silver coins can also be purchased as investments. Rolls and bags of up to $1,000 face value of circulated silver coins are available from coin and bullion dealers. As would be expected, nearly all of the coins in such bulk lots will be common dates from the 1960s (or, for silver dollars, Morgan dollars of 1921 and Peace dollars of 1922 and 1923).

POSTMASTER: PLEASE POST IN A CONSPICUOUS PLACE.—JAMES A. FARLEY, Postmaster General

UNDER EXECUTIVE ORDER OF THE PRESIDENT

issued April 5, 1933

all persons are required to deliver

ON OR BEFORE MAY 1, 1933

all GOLD COIN, GOLD BULLION, AND GOLD CERTIFICATES now owned by them to a Federal Reserve Bank, branch or agency, or to any member bank of the Federal Reserve System.

Executive Order

FORBIDDING THE HOARDING OF GOLD COIN, GOLD BULLION AND GOLD CERTIFICATES.

By virtue of the authority vested in me by Section 5(b) of the Act of October 6, 1917, as amended by Section 2 of the Act of March 9, 1933, entitled "An Act to provide relief in the existing national emergency in banking, and for other purposes", in which amendatory Act Congress declared that a serious emergency exists, I, Franklin D. Roosevelt, President of the United States of America, do declare that said national emergency still continues to exist and pursuant to said section do hereby prohibit the hoarding of gold coin, gold bullion, and gold certificates within the continental United States by individuals, partnerships, associations and corporations and hereby prescribe the following regulations for carrying out the purposes of this order:

Section 1. For the purposes of this regulation, the term "hoarding" means the withdrawal and withholding of gold coin, gold bullion or gold certificates from the recognized and customary channels of trade. The term "person" means any individual, partnership, association or corporation.

Section 2. All persons are hereby required to deliver on or before May 1, 1933, to a Federal reserve bank or a branch or agency thereof or to any member bank of the Federal Reserve System all gold coin, gold bullion and gold certificates now owned by them or coming into their ownership on or before April 28, 1933, except the following:

(a) Such amount of gold as may be required for legitimate and customary use in industry, profession or art within a reasonable time, including gold prior to refining and stocks of gold in reasonable amounts for the usual trade requirements of owners mining and refining such gold.

(b) Gold coin and gold certificates in an amount not exceeding in the aggregate $100.00 belonging to any one person; and gold coins having a recognized special value to collectors of rare and unusual coins.

(c) Gold coin and bullion earmarked or held in trust for a recognized foreign government or foreign central bank or the Bank for International Settlements.

(d) Gold coin and bullion licensed for other proper transactions (not involving hoarding) including gold coin and bullion imported for reexport or held pending action on applications for export licenses.

Section 3. Until otherwise ordered any person becoming the owner of any gold coin, gold bullion, or gold certificates after April 28, 1933, shall, within three days after receipt thereof, deliver the same in the manner prescribed in Section 2; unless such gold coin, gold bullion or gold certificates are held for any of the purposes specified in paragraphs (a), (b) or (c) of Section 2; or unless such gold coin or gold bullion is held for purposes specified in paragraph (d) of Section 2 and the person holding it is, with respect to such gold coin or bullion, a licensee or applicant for license pending action thereon.

Section 4. Upon receipt of gold coin, gold bullion or gold certificates delivered to it ... with Sections 2 or 3, the Federal reserve bank or member ba... ...ent amount of any other form of coin or curr...

Section 5. ...gold certificat... the provisions... districts and ...

Section 6. ...to the Presid... cases pay th... or gold certi... accordance w... protection, a... duction of ... purpose may ...

Section 7. ...certificates ... extraordina... his discreti... Application... dressed to ... bank. Ea... desired, th... certificates ... extension ...

Section ... empower... carry out... such offic... the Feder... in return... earmark... need for ... and (d) ...

Sectio... Order o... thereun... may be... director... such vi...

Thi...

Tu...

President Franklin D. Roosevelt.

For Further Information Cons...

GOLD CERTIFICATES may be identified b... appearing thereon. The serial number a... GOLD CERTIFICATE are printed in YELLO... CERTIFICATES with other issues which are ... GOLD CERTIFICATES. Federal Reserve Notes and United Stat...

"redeemable in gold" but are <u>not</u> "GOLD CERTIFICATES" and are <u>not</u> required to be surrendered

Special attention is directed to the exceptions allowed under Section 2 of the Executive Order

CRIMINAL PENALTIES FOR VIOLATION OF EXECUTIVE ORDER
$10,000 fine or 10 years imprisonment, or both, as provided in Section 9 of the order

Secretary of the Treasury.

Post Offices around the nation displayed flyers informing the public of the 1933 executive order for the surrender of gold and bullion.

How to Buy Rare Coins

Several good sources are available for purchasing rare coins. Each source has its advantages, and much depends on your experience and the type of material you're looking for.

Make sure your coin dealer is a member of the Professional Numismatists Guild or the American Numismatic Association.

Local Coin Dealers

A local dealer can be an excellent place to start your search for rare coins. You can examine the coins in person, and have your questions about the hobby answered. Establishing a relationship with someone you can trust can be your most valuable asset when buying rare coins. As recommended elsewhere in this book, look for dealers who are members of the American Numismatic Association (ANA) or the Professional Numismatists Guild (PNG). Both groups require dealers to follow a code of ethics, and you will have a third party to mediate any claims that may arise.

Internet

Ancient Rome meets 21st-century technology as collectors and investors browse hundreds of Internet sites that feature rare coins. Buyers can participate in auctions, peruse dealers' inventories, and gather tips on coin collecting.

Numismatic Conventions

Rare-coin conventions provide the chance to see thousands of coins and hundred of dealers in one place. A regional show is an excellent place to meet dealers and other fellow collectors. A national show offers an even larger selection of rare coins and most of the nation's most experienced dealers. Many also offer educational opportunities. The American Numismatic Association puts on three shows in various cities every year.

Whitman Coin and Collectibles Expos are held several times every year in Baltimore and Philadelphia. The Florida United Numismatists FUN Show is held twice yearly. Chances are, on any given weekend, there's a coin show within driving distance of your home.

A coin show is the ideal place to meet dozens of dealers with gold coins and bullion to sell.

AUCTIONS

When large collections are sold, the owners or their heirs typically contact one the larger numismatic auction houses. The auction firm will accept coins on consignment and sell them at public or Internet auction. Many of the nation's rarest and most expensive coins are sold in this manner. A quick glance through the *Guide Book of United States Coins* (the annual "Red Book" price guide) shows some of the nation's highest-dollar auctioneers: Bowers and Merena, Ira and Larry Goldberg, Heritage Auction Galleries, Sotheby's, Stack's-Bowers Numismatics, and Superior are some of the names most frequently seen among the Top 250 Coin Prices Realized at Auction (see the appendix of the *Guide Book*). More than 130 of the 250 highest prices are for gold coins alone, including federal, private, territorial, and colonial gold.

Auctioneer Christine Karstedt engages the audience at the final presentation of the Eliasberg Collection (2005). This series of sales featured the most valuable coin collection—including plenty of gold rarities—ever to cross the auction block.

Collecting rare gold and silver coins is an exciting and rewarding experience. Of all of the remnants of our history, perhaps none is more widely available, more affordable, and more interesting than rare coins. Nearly every other artifact of the past has all but disappeared, or is a priceless museum object. Sufficient quantities still exist to make coins affordable relics that are in reach of most collectors. Be careful—once you get started, it is easy to get hooked!

The $4 Stella was a gold coin suggested in the late 1870s by John A. Kasson, a former congressman from Iowa then serving as U.S. envoy extraordinary and minister plenipotentiary to Austria-Hungary. In theory the Stella would have been America's answer to the British sovereign, Italy's 20 lire, and other foreign gold coins popular in international trade. The coin never made it past the pattern stage. In 1879 several hundred were struck in gold, in two styles (Flowing Hair and Coiled Hair). A few dozen are known from 1880, as well. The 1880, Coiled Hair, type has approached $1 million at auction.

No. 18 among the top 250 coin prices realized at auction: an 1861 double eagle with a modified design by Anthony Pacquet. The so-called Pacquet Reverse (see example, right) has taller letters than the normal reverse (left) created by James Longacre. ($1,610,000)

You just bought an Indian Head gold half eagle for several hundred dollars. Is the coin authentic? Learn how to tell, and you'll save yourself the expense of later finding a fake—like the one pictured here—in your collection.

AVOIDING COUNTERFEIT
AND ALTERED COINS

Coin collectors occasionally find counterfeit gold coins, or coins that have been altered or changed so that they appear to be something other than what they really are. Any coin that does not seem to fit the description of similar pieces listed in a reference such as the *Guide Book of United States Coins* (the "Red Book") should be looked upon with suspicion. Experienced coin dealers can usually tell quickly whether a coin is genuine, and an ethical dealer would never knowingly sell fake coins to a collector. Coins bought from a nonprofessional source (in a flea market, for example, or from an unknown online seller) should be examined carefully.

You can minimize your risk of purchasing a spurious coin through the use of common sense and an elementary knowledge of the techniques used by counterfeiters. Keep in mind that the more popular a coin is among collectors and the public, the more likely it is that counterfeits and replicas will abound. Counterfeiters in Asia and elsewhere create fakes of a surprising variety of coins, most notably silver dollar types, but also smaller denominations and gold.

REPLICAS

Reproductions of famous and historical gold and silver coins have been distributed for decades by marketing firms and souvenir vendors. These pieces are often tucked away by the original recipients as curios, and later are found by others who believe they have discovered objects of great value. Most replicas are poorly made by the casting method, and are virtually worthless. They can sometimes be identified by a seam that runs around the edge of the piece where the two halves of the casting mold were joined together. Genuine specimens of extremely rare or valuable coins are almost never found in unlikely places.

COUNTERFEITS

For many centuries, counterfeiters have produced base-metal forgeries of gold and silver coins to deceive the public in the normal course of trade. These pieces are usually crudely made and easily detected on close examination. Crudely cast counterfeit copies of older coins are the most prevalent. These can usually be detected by the casting bubbles or pimples that can be seen with low-power magnification. Pieces struck from handmade dies are more deceptive, but the engravings do not match those of genuine U.S. Mint products.

More recently, as coin collecting has gained popularity and rare coin prices have risen, "numismatic" counterfeits have become more common. The majority of these are die-struck counterfeits that have been mass produced overseas since 1950. Forgeries exist of most U.S. gold coins dated between 1870 and 1933, as well as all issues of the gold dollar and three-dollar gold piece. Most of these are very well made, as they were intended to pass the close scrutiny of collectors. Fewer gold coins of earlier dates have been counterfeited, but false 1799 ten-dollar gold pieces and 1811 five-dollar coins have been made. Gold coins in less than Extremely Fine condition are seldom counterfeited.

Bust dollars (including those dated 1804), trade dollars, Morgan dollars, and several of the lower-mintage silver commemoratives have all been forged in quantity.

As good as gold? This 1908 Liberty Head half eagle is actually a counterfeit. The circles indicate areas of suspicion. (shown enlarged on the following page)

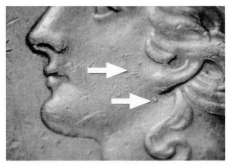 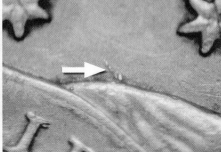

Notice the blemishes on the cheek and jaw. A spike jutting from Liberty's head is a telltale sign.

ALTERATIONS

Coins are occasionally altered by the addition, removal, or change of a design feature (such as a mintmark or date digit) or by the polishing, sandblasting, acid etching, toning, or plating of the surface of a genuine piece. Changes of this sort are usually done to deceive collectors. Among U.S. gold coins, only the 1927-D double eagle is commonly found with an added mintmark. On $2.50 and $5 gold coins, 1839 through 1856, New Orleans O mintmarks have been altered to C (for Charlotte, North Carolina) in a few instances.

Over a century ago, dishonest fraudsters gold-plated some 1883 Liberty Head nickels when the coins first came out. More than five million of the coins were made without the word CENTS on the reverse—just the Roman numeral V. Because the Liberty Head design was new and unfamiliar to the public, and because the five-cent nickel is about the same size as a half eagle, the gold-plated nickels could pass as $5 gold coins. A merchant, with just a quick glance at the Roman numeral V, might mistake the coin for a gold $5 piece and give $4.95 change for a 5¢ purchase.

A genuine high-grade 1927-D double eagle (like this one, from the Smithsonian's collection) could be worth close to $2 million. A counterfeit would only be worth the gold it's made from—assuming it contains any precious metal at all.

DETECTION

The best way to detect counterfeit coins is to compare suspected pieces with others of the same issue. Carefully check size, color, luster, weight, edge devices, and design details. Replicas generally have less detail than their genuine counterparts when studied under magnification. Modern struck counterfeits made to deceive collectors are an exception to this rule. Any questionable coin should be referred to an expert for verification.

Cast forgeries are usually poorly made and of incorrect weight. Base metal is often used in place of gold and silver, and the coins are lightweight and often incorrect in color and luster. Deceptive cast pieces have been made using real metal content and modern dental techniques, but these too usually vary in quality and color.

Detection of alterations sometimes involves comparative examination of the suspected areas of a coin (usually mintmarks and date digits) at magnification ranging from 10x to 40x.

Gold and silver coins of exceptional rarity or value should never be purchased without a written guarantee of authenticity. Professional authentication of rare coins for a fee is available with the services offered by commercial grading services, and by some coin dealers.

In the *United States Gold Counterfeit Detection Guide*, author Bill Fivaz writes, "A surprisingly large number of the United States gold pieces currently on the market are counterfeit. . . . Many of these counterfeit pieces have been produced overseas, and they usually contain gold of the proper weight and fineness." Fivaz offers several rules of thumb for identifying counterfeit gold coins, some of which are summarized here:

Weak, fat, mushy letters and devices. These often reveal a coin to be counterfeit. Authentic pieces should be sharp and crisp.

Weak, fat letters on a counterfeit quarter eagle.

Depression on a counterfeit gold eagle.

Repeating depressions. A depression that appears in the same place (often the fields) on several coins of the same series/date/mintmark likely is the result of contact marks that were on a genuine coin used to create a counterfeit die. "These should always be suspect," writes Fivaz, "especially when they are of the same texture as the rest of the field and have soft, rounded edges."

Tool marks. Many counterfeit Indian Head quarter eagles and half eagles have worm-like, raised tooling marks— often at the back of the Indian's neck or above the necklace. These come from the counterfeiter's attempts to finesse a false die.

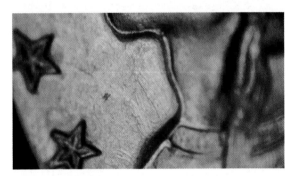

Tool marks on a counterfeit Indian Head quarter eagle.

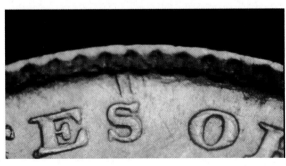

Spikes on a counterfeit gold coin.

Spikes. "In most cases," writes Fivaz, "these tool marks running from the dentils on a coin are a good indication that it is not a genuine piece. However, this characteristic should not be used exclusively."

Sunken letters or numbers. If the centers of a coin's letters or numbers appear to be depressed or concave, it is probably a counterfeit. Counterfeit 1811 Capped Bust half eagles are commonly found with this diagnostic.

Sunken date numerals on a counterfeit Capped Bust half eagle.

Irregular reeding on a counterfeit gold dollar.

Irregular edge. Irregular, uneven, or coarse reeding can reveal a coin to be a counterfeit. Also, test marks on the edge can be a tipoff, indicating that someone else, in the past, questioned the coin's authenticity.

Bubbles. Surface bubbles are the telltale sign of a cast counterfeit. Typically also the details will be very weak and ill-defined, and the color incorrect.

Bubbles on a counterfeit quarter eagle.

Color. Experienced collectors and gold-specialist dealers can usually tell, even at arm's length, if a coin is of the proper color for its date and mint. For example, branch-mint gold coins struck in Dahlonega and New Orleans often have a greenish hue, while those made in Charlotte usually have a reddish color.

"Spinning." Fivaz notes that some counterfeit Indian Head half eagles may "spin" when placed flat on a hard surface, due to one side being cup-shaped.

Mintmark. It is estimated that nearly 90% of counterfeit Liberty Head gold coins are Philadelphia fakes (with no mintmark).

It is essential to study as many authentic coins as possible in the series you wish to collect. Examine slabbed coins and note the crispness of their letters, numbers, and devices, their color and luster, and their surface qualities. Education is crucial to wise collecting and investing. The American Numismatic Association offers a Counterfeit Detection Course at its annual Summer Seminar (see money.org for details), as well as other educational opportunities at its shows. Hobby periodicals report on counterfeit coins, as well. The more you learn, the better equipped you will be to identify fraudulent coins that are less than they seem.

DIAMETERS OF GENUINE UNITED STATES GOLD COINS

Type	Diameter	Type	Diameter
Gold Dollar		**Half Eagle ($5)**	
1849–1854 (Liberty Head)	13 mm	1795–1807 (Capped Bust to Right)	~25 mm
1854–1889 (Indian Princess Head)	15 mm	1807–1812 (Capped Bust to Left)	~25 mm
1903–1922 (commemoratives)	15 mm	1813–1834 (Capped Head to Left)	~ 25 mm
		1834–1836 (Classic Head)	23.8 mm
Quarter Eagle ($2.50)		1837–1838 (Classic Head)	22.5 mm
1796–1807 (Capped Bust to Right)	~20 mm	1839–1908	
1808 (Capped Bust to Left)	~20 mm	(Liberty Head, all varieties)	21.6 mm
1821–1827 (Capped Head to Left,		1908–1929 (Indian Head)	21.6 mm
Large Diameter)	~18.5 mm	1986 to date (commemoratives)	21.6 mm
1829–1834 (Capped Head to Left,			
Reduced Diameter)	18.2 mm	**Eagle ($10)**	
1834–1839 (Classic Head)	18.2 mm	1795–1804 (Capped Bust to Right)	~33 mm
1840–1907 (Liberty Head, all	18 mm	1838–1907 (Liberty Head, all varieties)	27 mm
varieties)		1907–1933 (Indian Head)	27 mm
1908–1929 (Indian Head)	18 mm	1984 to date (commemoratives)	27 mm
$3 Gold Piece		**Double Eagle ($20)**	
1854–1889 (Indian Princess Head)	20.5 mm	1850–1907 (Liberty Head)	34 mm
		1907–1933 (Saint-Gaudens)	34 mm
$4 Stella (Pattern)			
1879–1880	22 mm		
1879–1880	22 mm		

Diameter Chart

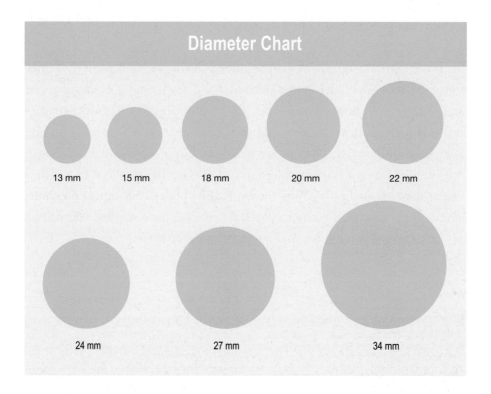

13 mm 15 mm 18 mm 20 mm 22 mm

24 mm 27 mm 34 mm

WEIGHTS AND TOLERANCES FOR UNITED STATES GOLD COINS

TYPE	GRAMS WT.	TOLERANCE	GRAINS WT.	TOLERANCE
Gold Dollar				
1849–1854 (Liberty Head)	1.672	0.016	25.80	0.25
1854–1889 (Indian Princess Head)	1.672	0.016	25.80	0.25
1903–1922 (commemoratives)	1.672	0.016	25.80	0.25
Quarter Eagle ($2.50)				
1796–1807 (Capped Bust to Right)	4.374		67.50	
1808 (Capped Bust to Left)	4.374		67.50	
1821–1827 (Capped Head to Left, Large Diameter)	4.374		67.50	
1829–1834 (Capped Head to Left, Reduced Diameter)	4.374		67.50	
1834–1836 (Classic Head)	4.180	0.008	64.50	0.13
1837–1839 (Classic Head)	4.180	0.016	64.50	0.25
1840–1907 (Liberty Head)	4.180	0.016	64.50	0.25
1908–1929 (Indian Head)	4.180	0.016	64.50	0.25

WEIGHTS AND TOLERANCES FOR UNITED STATES GOLD COINS

$3 Gold Piece

1854–1873 (Indian Princess Head)	5.015		77.40	
1873–1889 (Indian Princess Head)	5.015	0.016	77.40	0.25

$4 Stella (Pattern)

1879–1880	7.000		108.026	21.59

Half Eagle ($5)

1795–1807 (Capped Bust to Right)	8.748		135.00	
1807–1812 (Capped Bust to Left)	8.748		135.00	
1813–1834 (Capped Head to Left)	8.748		135.00	
1834–1836 (Classic Head)	8.359	0.017	129.00	0.26
1837–1838 (Classic Head)	8.359	0.016	129.00	0.25
1839–1849 (Liberty Head)	8.359	0.016	129.00	0.25
1849–1873 (Liberty Head)	8.359	0.032	129.00	0.50
1873–1929 (Liberty Head and Indian Head)	8.359	0.016	129.00	0.25
1986 to date (commemoratives)	8.359	0.042	129.00	0.65

Eagle ($10)

1795–1804 (Capped Bust to Right)	17.496		270.00	
1838–1849 (Liberty Head)	16.718	0.016	258.00	0.25
1849–1873 (Liberty Head)	16.718	0.032	258.00	0.50
1873–1933 (Liberty Head and Indian Head)	16.718	0.088	258.00	0.50
1984 to date (commemoratives)	16.718	0.088	258.00	1.36

Double Eagle ($20)

1850–1907 (Liberty Head)	33.436	0.032	516.00	0.50
1907–1933 (Saint-Gaudens)	33.436	0.032	516.00	0.50

Hundreds of professional coin dealers make the Whitman Coin and Collectibles Expo (held in Baltimore and Philadelphia) an ideal place to buy and sell precious metals.

DEAL WITH THE EXPERTS

66 All that glitters is not gold" is a familiar saying, and one that really does apply when buying and selling coins, ingots, and other precious-metal items. Counterfeits of United States and world coins abound. In some marketplaces, particularly overseas, they form the majority of gold coins (for example) offered by brokers. A significant number of gold coins offered in Internet auctions are counterfeit. Currently there is no meaningful policing of Internet sellers of fakes. Similarly, ingots can be falsified, by using metal other than gold, then plating it with gold and stamping marks on it.

"The 1907 High Relief Saint-Gaudens double eagle is a very famous and frequently counterfeited coin," writes Bill Fivaz in the *United States Gold Counterfeit Detection Guide*. "Check carefully any examples you intend to purchase." The coin shown here is actually a clever fake. The counterfeiter was proud enough of his fraudulent work to insert a tiny "signature"—the Greek letter omega—in the curl of the eagle's claw.

The circles highlight areas where tool marks and other telltale signs betray the false nature of this "coin." For more information on such clues, see chapter 7.

It takes an expert to determine counterfeits and it also takes an expert to assay gold or silver for its purity. What you see and expect might not be what you get.

Fortunately, there is some protection available for you. In the United States, members of the Professional Numismatists Guild (PNG, pngdealers.com) adhere to a code of ethics and guarantee the authenticity of the gold and other coins they sell. Members of the American Numismatic Association (ANA, money.org) also follow a professional code of ethics. Worldwide, the International Association of Professional Numismatists (IAPN, iapn-coins.org) has members who also abide by strict rules, including a lifetime guarantee of the authenticity of coins sold. If a dealer is a member of the ANA, the PNG, or the IAPN, this is a good indication for your business dealings.

Note that very few dealers in antiques and fine art are qualified to evaluate the authenticity of rare coins, and only a handful of art auction houses have a numismatic expert on staff. This applies to pawn shops, as well, and to flea-market vendors and others who may have coins for sale.

For valuable collector coins, certification by a third-party service such as ANACS, the Professional Coin Grading Service (PCGS), or the Numismatic Guaranty Corporation (NGC) is practically mandatory. There are other certification services as well, but these three are the main ones that

account for most of the rare-coin business. In order to ensure impartial service, their professional graders and authenticators are not active in the commercial aspects of the marketplace—they do not buy or sell coins professionally. This avoids any conflict of interest.

Professionally certified and graded coins are sealed in protective "slabs."

THE AMERICAN NUMISMATIC ASSOCIATION

The ANA is a nonprofit educational organization "dedicated to educating and encouraging people to study and collect money and related items." With nearly 33,000 members, the association serves the academic community, collectors, and the general public with an interest in numismatics. "The ANA helps all people discover and explore the world of money through its vast array of programs including its education and outreach, museum, library, publications, conventions, and seminars."

Web site: www.money.org

Web site features: Membership information; dealer directory; information on events and resources; history, FAQs, research tools; and more.

Contact:

ANA Headquarters

818 North Cascade Avenue

Colorado Springs, CO 80903

Telephone: 719-632-2646

Fax: 719-634-4085

Email: ana@money.org

Coins should be held by their edges, not gripped by front and back.
This helps avoid fingerprints, which lower a rare coin's value.

THE PROFESSIONAL NUMISMATISTS GUILD

The PNG is a nonprofit organization "composed of the world's top rare coin, paper money, and precious metals experts. As numismatic professionals, our primary mission is to make the hobby safe for collectors and investors by maintaining rigid standards of excellence for our member dealers." The average PNG dealer has more than 25 years of experience and more than $250,000 verified in numismatic assets.

Web site: www.pngdealers.com

Web site features: Dealer directory; "Collector Bill of Rights"; information on grading services; a rare coin primer, articles; fraud alerts; an "eBay Survival Guide"; and more.

Contact:

> Robert Brueggeman, Executive Director
> 3950 Concordia Lane
> Fallbrook, CA 92028
> Telephone: 760-728-1300
> Fax: 760-728-8507
> Email: info@pngdealers.com

THE INTERNATIONAL ASSOCIATION OF PROFESSIONAL NUMISMATISTS

The IAPN defines itself as a nonprofit organization of more than 110 of the leading international numismatic firms. The association was founded in Geneva, Switzerland, in 1951. Its objectives are "the development of a healthy and prosperous numismatic trade conducted according to the highest standards of business ethics and commercial practice."

Web site: www.iapn-coins.org

Web site features: List of member firms; information on committees, publications, press releases, and general numismatics; calendar of events and meetings.

Contact:

General Secretary Jean-Luc Van der Schueren

14, Rue de la Bourse, B-1000 Bruxelles

Telephone: +32-2-513 3400

Fax: +32-2-512 2528

Email: iapnsecret@iapn-coins.org

The Austrian Mint offers popular gold coins for collecting and investment. (shown 1.5x actual size)

ANACS

ANACS began in 1972 as part of the American Numismatic Association, dedicated to certifying the authenticity of submitted coins. This was in response to a flood of counterfeit and altered coins in the hobby. Later, in addition to authenticating coins, ANACS began grading them. In 1989 ANACS started encapsulating graded coins in tamper-resistant plastic holders. In 1990 the company was sold by the ANA, and since then it has been a private commercial firm, continuing its work in grading and authenticating coins.

Web site: www.anacs.com

Web site features: Information on services and products; hobby articles; spot metal prices; FAQs; special offers; coin-show schedule.

Contact:

> PO Box 6000
> Englewood, CO 80155
> Telephone: 800-888-1861
> Fax: 303-339-3450
> Email: CustomerService@anacs.com

NUMISMATIC GUARANTY CORPORATION OF AMERICA (NGC)

NGC was founded in 1987 as a third-party grading and authentication firm.

Web site: www.ngccoin.com

Web site features: Information on services and products; numismatic headlines; coin image galleries; spot metal prices; collector advisories; research articles; and more.

Contact:

PO Box 4776

Sarasota, FL 34230

Telephone: 800-NGC-COIN

Fax: 941-360-2553

Email: info@ngccoin.com

PROFESSIONAL COIN GRADING SERVICE (PCGS)

PCGS was founded in 1986 as a third-party grading and authentication firm.

Web site: www.pcgs.com

Web site features: Information on services and products; a coin price guide; numismatic articles and image library; videos; spot metal prices; and more.

Contact:

PO Box 9458

Newport Beach, CA 92658

Telephone: 800-447-8848

Fax: 941-360-2553

Email: info@pcgs.com

Exterior of "The Castle" (the original Smithsonian Institution Building), in Washington, DC. The Smithsonian is home to the National Numismatic Collection, which contains many of the greatest American gold coins ever minted.

MORE RESOURCES

ADDRESSES OF WORLD MINTS, CENTRAL BANKS, AND AGENCIES

Many of the international web sites listed have links to English-language versions.

Austria
Austrian Mint AG
Am Heurmarkt 1, 1031
Vienna, Austria
Web site: www.austrian-mint.com

Australia
Royal Australian Mint
Denison Street
Deakin, Canberra
ACT 2600, Australia
Web site: www.ramint.gov.au

Belgium
Royal Belgian Mint
Boulevard Pacheco 32
B-1000 Bruxelles, Belgium
Web site: www.royalmint.be

Canada
Royal Canadian Mint
PO Box 457
Station A, Ottawa, Ontario
KIN 8V5, Canada
Web site: www.mint.ca

China, People's Republic of
China Gold Coin Inc. (CGCI)
18/5, Agricultural Bank of China
No. 188 West Liberation Road
Shenzhen, Post Code 518001,
China
Web site: www.chngc.net

PBC – People's Bank of China
32 Chengfang Street
Xi Cheng District
Beijing, Post Code 100800, China
Web site: www.pbc.gov.cn

China, Republic of
Central Mint of China
577, Jhensing Road

Kweishan Taoyuan, Taiwan, ROC
Web site: www.cmc.gov.tw

France
Paris Mint, Monnaie de Paris
11 Quai de Conti
75270 Paris Cedex 06, France
Web site: www.monnaiedeparis.fr

Germany
Verkaufsstelle fur
Sammlermunzen der
Bundesrepublik
Bahnhofstrasse 16-18
D-6380 Bad Homburg 1,
Germany
Web site: www.bwpv.de

Great Britain
The British Royal Mint
Llantrisant, Pontyclun
Mid Glamorgan, Wales, CF7
8YT, UK
Web site: www.royalmint.com

Israel
Israel Government Coins and
Medals Corporation
POB 7900
Jerusalem 91078, Israel
Web site: www.isragift.co.il

Mexico
Banco de Mexico
Division de Colleccion
Numismatica
K312, Aptdo 98
Bis Col. Centro Mexico, DF
06059, Mexico
Web site: www.banxico.org.mx

Poland
Polish State Mint, Mennica

Panstwowa SA
21 Pereca Street
00-958 Warsaw, Poland
Web site: www.mennica.com.pl

Portugal
Casa de Moeda
Av. Dr. Antonio Jose de Almeida
1092 Lisbon, Codex, Portugal
Web site: www.incm.pt

Russia
Bank of Russia
Emission and Cash Department
12 Neglinnaya Str.
107016 Moscow, Russia
Web site: www.cbr.ru

South Africa
South African Mint
Old Johannesburg Road
Gateway, Centurion, South Africa
Web site: www.samint.za

Spain
Spanish Royal Mint
Jorge Juan 106, 28009 Jimenez
Madrid, Spain
Web site: www.fnmt.es

Switzerland
Banque Nationale Suisse
Bernastrasse 28, CH-3003
Berne, Switzerland
Web site: www.swissmint.ch

United States of America
U.S. Mint, Customer Service
Center
801 9th Street NW
Washington DC 20220
Web site: www.usmint.gov

ADDRESSES OF
FAMOUS GOLD COIN COLLECTIONS

NATIONAL NUMISMATIC COLLECTION

The National Numismatic Collection (NNC) of the Smithsonian Institution is the largest numismatic collection in North America, and one of the largest in the world. It is located in the National Museum of American History, Behring Center. The NNC holds about 1.6 million objects, including more than 450,000 coins, medals and decorations, highlighting the entire numismatic history of mankind. It is home to the greatest collection of U.S. gold coins in the world.

National Numismatic Collection
Smithsonian Institution
National Museum of Modern History, Behring Center
MRC 513, PO Box 37012
Capital Gallery, Suite 6001
Washington DC 20013-7012
Web site: www.americanhistory.si.edu/collections/numismatics/

Only one surviving example exists of the 1797 Heraldic Eagle $5 gold coin with 16 stars on the obverse. This unique piece of American history resides in the Smithsonian's National Numismatic Collection.

AMERICAN NUMISMATIC ASSOCIATION EDWARD C. ROCHETTE MONEY MUSEUM

The museum of the ANA includes exhibits in three main galleries, where visitors can explore spectacular rarities and learn about American and world history as seen through money. The multimedia Bass Gallery houses the Harry W. Bass Collection, a comprehensive collection of American gold coins, experimental pattern coins, and paper money. The main level features a new exhibit every year designed to appeal to a wide variety of interests, including history, art, archaeology, banking and economics, and coin collecting. The Maynard Sundman–Littleton Gallery and the Whitman Publishing Gallery on the museum's lower level also feature new exhibits every year, illuminating aspects of numismatics and collecting designed to appeal to collectors and the general public. The museum's collection holds more than 250,000 objects encompassing the history of numismatics from the earliest invention of money to the modern day—paper money, coins, tokens, medals, and traditional money from all over the world.

818 North Cascade Avenue
Colorado Springs CO 80903
On the campus of Colorado College, adjacent to the Colorado Springs Fine Arts Center.
Web site: www.money.org
Telephone: 800-367-9723

AMERICAN NUMISMATIC SOCIETY

The numismatic collection of the ANS holds approximately 800,000 coins and related objects. It is of international caliber, on par with the largest state collections of Europe. Abounding in both large study collections and great rarities, the Society's cabinets are particularly strong in ancient Greek coinage; Roman Republican period issues; Islamic issues; Far Eastern, particularly Chinese; Latin American; and United States, both colonial series and federal issues, as well as private coinages.

American Numismatic Society
75 Varick Street, Floor 11
New York NY 10013
Web site: www.numismatics.org/Collections/Collections
Telephone: 212-571-4470

The collection of the American Numismatic Society is famous for its ancient coins, as well as world and American.

CREDITS AND ACKNOWLEDGMENTS

The **Austrian Mint** shared images of gold coins. Special thanks to **Q. David Bowers** for writing the foreword to this book. **Arthur L. Friedberg** (Coin and Currency Institute, Clifton, New Jersey), editor of *A Catalog of Modern World Coins, 1850–1964*, contributed observations on world gold coins. **Gainesville Coins** (Gainesville, Florida) provided gold coins for photography. **Christian Jansky** provided the image on page 23. **Dwight Manley** and the **California Gold Marketing Group** provided illustrations of treasure from the SS *Central America*. **Mid-American Rare Coin Gallery** (Lexington, Kentucky) provided coins for photography. **Tom Mulvaney** (Lexington, Kentucky) photographed various gold coins and provided other images. **Kirsten Petersen** of the Austrian Mint assisted in image gathering. **SilverTowne** (Winchester, Indiana) provided gold coins for photography. The **Smithsonian Institution** (Washington, DC) provided photographs of several U.S. gold coins. **Stack's-Bowers Numismatics** (New York City and Wolfeboro, New Hampshire) provided photographs of gold coins, and other imagery. **Twery's Estate Buyers** (Greenacres, Florida) provided an image. Certain modern coin images are courtesy of the **United States Mint.** Portions of this book's text were modified with permission from *Gold: Everything You Need to Know to Buy and Sell Today* (Jeff Garrett and Q. David Bowers).

ABOUT THE FOREWORD WRITER

Legendary coin dealer, auctioneer, and researcher Q. David Bowers has served as president of both the American Numismatic Association and of the Professional Numismatists Guild; is a recipient of the highest honor bestowed by the ANA (the Farran Zerbe Award); was the first ANA member to be named Numismatist of the Year (1995); in 2005 was given the Lifetime Achievement Award; and has

Q. David Bowers.

been inducted into the ANA Numismatic Hall of Fame. Bowers has received the Professional Numismatists Guild's prestigious Founder's Award, and more "Book of the Year Award" and "Best Columnist" honors of the Numismatic Literary Guild than any other writer. He is the author of more than 50 books, hundreds of catalogs, and several thousand articles including columns in *Coin World, Paper Money,* and *The Numismatist.* He is chairman emeritus of Stack's Bowers Galleries and numismatic director for Whitman Publishing, and serves as research editor of the *Guide Book of United States Coins.*